Women, Family, and Community in Colonial America: Two Perspectives

The *Women & History* series:

- *Beautiful Merchandise: Prostitution in China 1860 - 1936,* by Sue Gronewold

- *The Empire of the Mother: American Writing about Domesticity 1830 - 1860,* by Mary P. Ryan

- *Women, Family, and Community in Colonial America: Two Perspectives,* by Alison Duncan Hirsch and Linda Speth, with an Introduction by Carol Berkin

Forthcoming:

- *Votes and More for Women: Suffrage and After in Connecticut,* by Carole Nichols, with an Introduction by Lois Banner

- *A New Song: Celibate Women in the First Three Christian Centuries,* by JoAnn McNamara

- *"Dames Employees": The Feminization of Postal Work in Nineteenth-Century France,* by Susan Bachrach

- *Women in the Enlightenment,* by Margaret Hunt, Margaret Jacob, Phyllis Mack, and Ruth Perry, with a Foreword by Ruth Graham

22.00

Women, Family, and Community in Colonial America: Two Perspectives

Linda E. Speth
Alison Duncan Hirsch
with an introduction by Carol Berkin

Copublished by
The Institute for Research in History and The Haworth Press, Inc.

74982

Women, Family, and Community in Colonial America: Two Perspectives has also been published as *Women & History*, Number 4, Winter 1982.

The Haworth Press, Inc., 28 East 22 Street, New York, NY 10010

Library of Congress Cataloging in Publication Data

Speth, Linda.
    Women, family, and community in colonial America.

    (Women & history ; no. 4)
    Includes bibliographical references.
        1. Married women—Virginia—History. 2. Wills—Virginia—History.
3. Dower—Virginia—History. 4. Trials (Divorce)—Connecticut—History.
I. Hirsch, Alison Duncan. II. Title. III. Series.
KF521.S63   1983   346.7301'34   82-23326
ISBN 0-86656-191-9   347.306134

Women, Family, and Community in Colonial America: Two Perspectives

Women & History
Number 4

CONTENTS

INTRODUCTION

Historians of colonial women have found legal sources and documents to be a mixed blessing: while commanding and demanding our attention, these records have not yielded up their secrets as easily as we might have wished. Lacking a Rosetta Stone, scholars have had to rely on a trial and error method. Nonetheless, legal sources promise to tell us more about women's status and role in colonial society than any other historical source.

We already know that the law itself is not descriptive of reality but proscriptive. Laws show what a society wishes to be, what it aspires to—or at least what those in power aspire to for themselves and for others. While reconstructing the legal paradigms is essential, it has proven disastrous to confuse them with reality, especially in the case of colonial women. Despite their legally circumscribed and subordinate status, women were not as helpless to shape their lives as they appeared to be in the law.

In addition, the discovery and explication of colonial women's legal status has been complicated by the existence of different patterns in each colony. Thus legal historians have had to constantly revise, correct, or qualify their descriptions of the legal status of women as they moved from Quaker records in Pennsylvania, to Puritan-inspired records in Massachusetts, or to Virginia and New York laws. This task of reconstruction has been so tortuous and has required such painstaking scholarship that we are naturally loathe to dismiss our accomplishment as no more than a starting point.

Clearly, however, historians such as Marylynn Salmon, Lois Carr and Lorena Walsh, and Gwen Gampel have gone beyond these early stages of legal excavation and labeling. They, like the two young historians in this volume, have sought to discover social realities rather than proscriptions; to measure and analyze the gap between the ideal and the real; to explore the impact of law on women's lives, and conversely, the impact of women's lives on the development of the law; to trace the connections between economic exigency and legal innovation; to exploit the legal records so that they yield up new information and insight into the daily experiences

1

of colonial women; and finally, to effectively join issues of women's legal status to other significant issues in women's history.

The two essays in this volume go far in advancing our understanding of colonial women, as well as illustrating how to use legal sources effectively. They reflect the diversity of approach to legal sources and show us how to enhance the value of this kind of documentation by intelligently combining it with material on demography, economic organization of colonial society, and the structure of the colonial family.

In "More Than Her 'Thirds': Wives and Widows in Colonial Virginia," Linda Speth analyzes a collection of 394 wills from three Virginia counties in order to discover general patterns of behavior among rural women and men regarding property. Throughout her essay, she has four central questions in mind: first, to what degree did Virginia husbands and fathers conform to legal tradition regarding inheritance patterns, and in what significant ways did their practice diverge? Second, what do their wills tell us about how women were regarded and treated by men? Third, to what degree did women actually acquire and control property, and under what set of circumstances? Finally, what patterns of behavior emerged among women who, as widows, acquired and controlled property?

These questions directly address one of the key debates in colonial women's history: to what extent did colonial women enjoy autonomy and power within their society? The question has been aphorized as "Golden Age or Grim Patriarchy?" and it has become our own phoenix, rising from the ashes of endless debate. Its survival both irritates and fascinates us. It is a major strength of Speth's article that she eschews polemics, does not marshal her evidence on one side or the other, but explores Virginia realities of inheritance and ensuing economic power with balanced judgment and with care.

The picture that emerges from Speth's deft examination of the wills and her interjection of other sources is this: Virginia men freely diverged from the inheritance patterns suggested by law because demographic and life cycle factors (the realities of their lives) propelled them to innovation and to an active rather than a passive attitude toward the law. These men perceived their wives as competent to control their estates and to wield economic power. But young men with young wives and children were more likely to transfer this authority to their widows than older men with older wives and adult children. Thus, an ironic reversal occurred based on sex: male opportunity for autonomy and authority increased with age in colonial Virginia; female opportunity for autonomy and authority decreased with age.

Speth's widows proved self-reliant and able managers of their property and wealth. The overwhelming majority did not remarry. Most chose to run their farms alone, without the aid of an adult son or a male friend. In fact, two-thirds lived in homes without adult male children. These widows sometimes delayed giving children their inheritance, either to maintain their parental authority or to prevent family wealth from reaching the hands of a daughter's husband. Clearly, these women understood how to wield economic power for personal and familial ends.

Speth's rural Virginia society was neither egalitarian nor highly repressive for women. Her study affirms our belief that social realities are more complex and more dynamic than ideologies, present or past.

Alison Duncan Hirsch's essay, "The Thrall Case: A Family Crisis in Eighteenth-Century Connecticut," contrasts sharply with Speth's in its methodology and its intent. Hirsch has chosen to reconstruct a family crisis from the records of a single divorce case. Her effort is not merely descriptive, however. Framing the story are three important questions: first, what can certain types of court records tell us about female and male *affective* relationships as well as formal relationships? Second, how and with what consequences did these colonists test social and behavioral boundaries through their courts? Finally, how did the relationship between the family and the community create a public role for women?

In asking this last question, Hirsch returns us to the issue of women's power within the colonial society. For what Hirsch suggests is this: in a world where the family and community are closely linked by ties of blood and marriage, and where the family is the core unit in creating a well-ordered community, a woman's actions and decisions have the power to disrupt or sustain that order.

Hirsch's essay displays a fine sensitivity to what court records can tell historians if they are properly attentive. Divorce records, Hirsch notes, capture the most ordinary stuff of daily life, scenes and dialogues and attitudinal clues so mundane that no diarist or letter-writer would mention them. She skillfully lifts these revelations from the web of legal testimony. Her success urges others to work with these documents in a similar way.

Carol Berkin

MORE THAN HER "THIRDS": WIVES AND WIDOWS IN COLONIAL VIRGINIA

Linda E. Speth

Introduction

Traditionally, historians have maintained that the seventeenth and eighteenth centuries constituted a golden age for the American woman. Then, it is argued, her legal, economic, and social status was far higher in America than in England; it was after the American Revolution that she lost ground in both the public and private spheres.[1] This view is currently being debated and reevaluated as scholars begin to use a wide variety of sources, such as church, court, and legal records, to describe the experiences of women who were not part of the colonial elite. In addition, sophisticated legal-historical studies by such scholars as Lois Carr, Lorena Walsh, Marylynn Salmon, Joan R. Gunderson, Gwen Gampel, and Joan Hoff Wilson have begun to define the complex legal, demographic, and economic factors that converged to influence women's lives in specific colonies.[2]

However, historians interested in studying the women of eighteenth-century Virginia face a serious problem in obtaining sources. Colonial Virginia had high illiteracy rates, and documents such as letters and diaries that might tell us much about women's aspirations, behavior, or beliefs simply do not exist in sufficient numbers.[3] In addition, many of the local church and court records of the various Virginia counties were destroyed during the American Revolution and the Civil War.

Despite the relative scarcity of historical sources, one area of

Linda E. Speth received a M.A. degree in History at Utah State University in 1980. Her other publications include works on western resource management and administration as well as "The Married Women's Property Acts, 1839–1865: Reform, Reaction, or Revolution?" in *Women and the Law: A Social-Historical Perspective* (Cambridge, 1982). She is currently Director, Utah State University Press.

Virginia does contain records that reveal significant details and provide insights to the lives of eighteenth-century women. Amelia,
Prince Edward, and Mecklenburg counties, areas of the eighteenth-
century piedmont, have a complete run of court records. The historian can use probate and tax records to indicate patterns of behavior, to identify male attitudes about women, and even to suggest the
measure and quality of female participation within the family and
the larger agricultural community. In the absence of such traditional
sources as letters and diaries, the 394 wills of the three counties are
often the only existing personal statements made by male colonists
about women, and by a few women about themselves. By analyzing
the probate records in this area of Southside Virginia, one can isolate and identify the broad economic and demographic factors that
influenced a woman's role and status.

Herbert G. Gutman has perceptively noted in his work on the
black family that both status and role must be considered when
studying minorities. The two are not always the same, and the roles
a member of a minority group assumes often differ in scope and
design from the subordinant and limited status a dominant society
assigns. Although the legal and social structure of America did not
recognize the existence of black families, black kin relationships, or
black marriages, the slaves created and sustained viable familial
relationships. For scholars to study a minority as only passive vic-
tims of regulation gives an incomplete perspective.[4]

Gutman's insight is no less valid for studying another minority—
the women of colonial Virginia. The legal code of the colony and
the few literary sources that have survived can help define the status
of the Southern woman. But the probate records of the three Southside counties reveal that, although the legal and religious institutions
of colonial Virginia relegated women to the home, many Southside
women, at least in widowhood, achieved a considerable measure of
personal power and responsibility. These legal records, particularly
the wills written in the years prior to the Revolution, offer valuable
insights into women's access to property, and, as historians such as
Lois Carr, Lorena Walsh, James Deen, and Daniel Scott Smith have
demonstrated, suggest how members of the colonial family regarded
each other.

Wills serve yet another function; they document the transfer of
authority from one individual to another. James K. Somerville, in
his study of Salem women, observes that both the transfer of prop-

erty and authority must be considered in determining whether or not "women were treated as responsible, purposeful individuals."[5]

A study of probate and other manuscript court records can thus be very useful to women's historians in their attempts to answer some of the thornier questions of women's history. At the very least, they give us the opportunity to more deeply explore the fabric of the female experience in the Old Dominion.

The Legal Status of Women in Eighteenth-Century Virginia

Like her male counterpart, a woman's position within Virginia society depended on both her class and race. The wife of a wealthy planter enjoyed more leisure time and greater social prestige than the wife of a frontier farmer, and both their lives differed radically from the activities of the female slave who served them. Appropriate feminine behavior and dress were, in part, dictated by an awareness of one's station and rank in society. In 1772 Landon Carter, a wealthy planter, was disturbed to see the wife of one of his plantation managers "act the part of a fine lady in all of her traveling apparel with at least 2 maids besides her own girl to get the dinner and wait upon her."[6]

The manner books and morality tracts of the period emphasized that marriage and motherhood constituted woman's God-ordained function, her natural and inevitable sphere. Proscriptive literature directed toward women as well as religious sermons reasoned that Eve's initial transgression in the Garden of Eden had caused the Almighty to place women under the authority of their husbands and to order women to bear and rear their husbands' children.[7] The notion that the household and the family were woman's sole preserve pervaded contemporary literature, and was reinforced by the Anglican Church, the officially established church in Virginia.

Women's status within the family and larger society was also determined by the legal institutions of colonial Virginia. Both English common-law tradition and colonial statute defined a patriarchal milieu in which women, particularly wives, were regarded as passive, dependent, and subordinate members of society. Although scholars are currently debating the extent to which the early settlers transplanted the English common-law tradition,[8] the Virginia lawmakers followed the basic outlines of that tradition as it affected women. In both England and Virginia, a woman's legal status, her civil obligations and privileges were to a large extent determined by her marital status. For purposes of private law, a single woman, or *feme sole,* had the same legal privileges as a man. A single, adult woman could enter into contracts, sue her debtors, and dispose of her personal and real property by either will or deed. Her relative legal freedom in controlling her economic assets ended, however, at the moment of her marriage. For all practical, economic purposes, once she married she became a legal nonentity. Her husband not only assumed her legal privileges and duties but certain rights to her property as well.[9]

The married woman, or *feme covert,* lost complete and total control over her personal property. Her livestock, jewels, furniture, even the clothes on her back belonged to her husband. He could sell her personal property or give it away if he so wished; the laws of the colony gave him the power to do so and the wife possessed no legal right to object. Furthermore, any wages she earned or any personal property she inherited during the course of the marriage also belonged totally to her husband. Although a man could not sell his wife's real estate without her consent, he did gain the use of it during the marriage. Thus, without consulting his wife, a man could decide what to plant and where to build fences or barns—on "her" land. All rents or profits accruing from such use belonged to the husband alone, and the law did not recognize a married woman's economic interest in her own property. Even at her death, the husband remained in control of her land if they had children. He became a tenant for life, and at his death the land reverted to the couple's children. At no time during her married life did the common law recognize a wife's control of her real estate.[10]

Under the common law, the *feme covert*'s economic and proprietary incapacities were striking. Technically, she could not enter into a contract, execute a deed, or make a will unless she had her husband's permission. Historian Mary Beard has argued that equity, a separate system of jurisprudence, mitigated the traditional common-law disabilities associated with coverture and led to widespread economic independence for married women.[11] Equity, both in England and Virginia, provided a loophole for the *feme covert.* For example, a married woman could escape some of her legal and economic incapacities via the creation of a separate estate, whereby her property was removed from her spouse's control. Recently the first systematic investigation of colonial equity procedures and their impact on married women has questioned that equity ameliorated the legal and economic dependency of married women. Marylynn Salmon found in colonial Pennsylvania that equitable procedures were used to protect family property from a daughter's spouse, rather than to enhance a married woman's legal or economic independence.[12] A similar conclusion seems warranted for eighteenth-century Virginia. In 1773, for example, Samuel Chapman of Amelia County wrote: "I give to my loving Daughter Unity Loving a Negro girl Named Jude, and if her Husband should by any lewd way by gameing or any other way Satisfy any of his Debts part with the said Negro girl Jude she shall be Immediately Recovered by the Heir at Law of My Own Body . . ."[13] The issue was protection of family property rather than economic independence or control for Unity Loving.

The common law itself recognized the *feme covert*'s vulnerable position, and in both England and Virginia lawmakers provided for the wife's minimal economic protection. In 1748 the Burgesses began to revise existing statutes and stipulated the interests of both husband and wife in property, especially land. Although the husband still retained complete control over his wife's personal property, an Act of October, 1748, ordered that if he wished to sell or convey any of his wife's land, he had to obtain her written permission. To make sure that she consented voluntarily and not because her husband forced her, the lawmakers provided that a woman had to be examined privately, apart from her husband, by the justices of the local county court. Only after they determined that she was agreeable to the sale of her own land or the land in which she had a future interest, could the legal transfer be completed. The Burgesses even ordered that if a woman was too ill to travel to court, the justices of the peace would go to her to conduct the private examination.[14] The Virginia effort to prevent possible coercion of wives was not a colonial innovation; Frederic Maitland and Frederick Pollock, English legal scholars, note that the private examination of the wife in cases involving the conveyance of land was an established feature of the English common law as early as the thirteenth century.[15]

Other statutory Virginia laws establishing minimal protection for wives dealt primarily with the rights of widows; again these laws, in broad terms, followed English precedents. For centuries the most important legal and economic right an English wife possessed was her dower. In 1662 the Virginia Burgesses ordered that when a man died without leaving a will, his widow received a full third of his estate. In 1705 and 1748 they elaborated further on the dower principle, ensuring a wife the minimum economic requirements for her subsistence. Basically the act of 1748 was a recasting of the 1705 enactment; it specifically and in great detail set forth the wife's dower interest in different types of her late husband's property. When a man died intestate, statutory law guaranteed the widow a life interest in one-third of her husband's land and slaves. Although English common-law dower technically refers only to rights in realty, the colonists used the term broadly to include a woman's interest in her husband's personal property as well. In this respect the Virginia widow during the eighteenth century had access to a greater share of her husband's estate than her English counterpart.[16]

The Burgesses in Williamsburg felt that a widow's dower provided the basic minimum necessary to support herself and her children. To ensure that she received her "thirds," they ordered that her husband could not sell his land in which she possessed a future right of dower without her consent. The necessary private examination had to be conducted and recorded to make sure that she consented willingly. Futhermore, they made it difficult for a husband to deprive his wife of her minimum by giving her the right to contest his will. If the wife was unhappy or dissatisfied with the bequest her husband left her, she could appear in court, renounce the will, and claim her common-law "thirds." The justices of the county court would then appoint a commission to divide the testator's estate and ensure that the wife received her dower.[17]

The legislators transplanted English common-law dower because dower reduced the chance that the widow would become a public expense and drain colonial tax revenues. Virginia, like England, had a public welfare system of sorts, and the aged, the infirm, and the very poor could receive aid from their local parishes. But the family, not the larger society, had the primary responsibility for caring for its less fortunate members. By preserving and guarding common-law dower, the Virginia Burgesses placed the burden of supporting a widow squarely on the shoulders of her husband. Only when a man himself was too poor to provide for his widow would the community contribute to her maintenance.

Even though the Virginia husband had to give his wife her dower and could not sell her land without her permission, he still retained considerable control over the economic resources of the family unit. Moreover both colonial statutes and English common law gave him almost complete power over his wife's person and supervised intimate aspects of the relationship between husband and wife, as well.

In 1736, George Webb, concerned about the lack of legal education and knowledge within the colony, published a handbook for local justices that summarized both the laws of Virginia and aspects of the common law that applied to the colony. In it he noted that the Virginia wife was totally "under her Husband's Power."[18] The husband's absolute authority over his wife included the legal privilege of beating her,[19] and local justices interfered in these private "domestic matters" only if the husband was unduly brutal. At the beginning of the eighteenth century, Elizabeth Wildy complained to the Northumberland County Court that her husband not only whipped and maimed her but also held her in the fire until her clothes burned. The justices felt that in this case the husband had exceeded his right of "reasonable chastisement" and ordered him to appear in court and explain.[20]

The Burgesses enacted several laws upholding the general principle of the husband's total authority within the family circle that ignored the rights of wives and mothers. For example, in 1748 they passed a law that gave the husband sole power to appoint guardians for his children and to apprentice them out to learn a trade while their mother was still alive. The statute was within the tradition of the common law that gave total authority to the husband and father; the mother possessed no legal say in her children's upbringing, and the English jurist, Sir William Blackstone, argued that she was entitled only to their love and respect.[21]

As Julia Cherry Spruill has pointed out in her classic study of Southern colonial women, the general concept of male authority was so strongly embedded in eighteenth-century society that the Virginia lawmakers upheld it even in the face of their own religious prejudices. In 1703 Ann Walker, an Anglican, complained to the Virginia Council that her Quaker husband had educated their children in his religion. The councillors, all members of the established Anglican Church, and men who had passed laws demonstrating a strong hostility to Quakers, told Ann not to interfere with her children's religious training. They suggested instead of causing domestic discord she ought to be properly grateful that her husband allowed her to practice her own Anglican faith.[22]

The general principle of male authority and female subordination was even reflected and embodied in criminal matters. Although hanging was the traditional punishment for homicide, the wife who murdered her spouse, like the slave who killed his master, was subject to a more gruesome form of execution. According to the common law, the guilty wife or slave was charged with petit treason and could be burned alive for the offense against constituted authority.[23]

Although both English and Virginia law restricted the married woman's economic and personal autonomy, certain institutional limitations hampered the Virginia wife more than her English counterpart. In England it was possible to break the spiritual contract of marriage in an ecclesiastical court. This religious institution would grant total divorce, *a vinculo matrimoni,* if the petitioner were wealthy enough or demonstrated a canonical impediment to the marriage. In cases of either "intolerable ill temper or adultery" it could also order a "separation from bed and board," *a mensa et thoro.*[24] But the settlers had not established ecclesiastical courts in Virginia. Without this agency, there was no colonial tribunal, civil or religious, that could grant a total divorce. Occasionally, a local county court could grant a legal separation. But worried about their jurisdiction and hesitant about interfering in a religious matter, the Virginia courts did so only in extreme and unusual circumstances.[25] For most women of eighteenth-century Virginia, the legal and religious ties that bound them to their spouses would not be broken by adultery, physical abuse, or even desertion. The marriage contract and the husband's power and authority could end only with death.

Virginia women, of course, played no part in formulating the laws which deprived wives of economic independence and personal authority, and which made them dependent on their husbands. In 1699 the Burgesses formally denied women the right to vote when they passed an act to prevent the "undue election" of legislators. The lawmakers ordered that "No woman sole or covert, infants under the age of twenty one years, or recusant convert being freeholders shall be enabled to give a vote or have a voice in the election of burgesses . . ."[26] Neither Catholics, children, nor women could vote in colonial Virginia.

Virginia statutory law and the English common-law tradition denied women a voice within the political arena, limited the participation of married women within the economic sector, and recognized the husband's authority within the intimate confines of the family circle. Both law and religion, then, agreed that woman's proper sphere was in the family under the dominion of her husband.

Although Virginia law restricted married women, legal codes do not describe the full parameters of feminine access to property and authority within the most basic institution of colonial society—the family. Recent studies by Joan R. Gunderson and Gwen Gampel have begun to show how colonial law operated in practice, how the totally restrictive image of coverture was not totally accurate for either eighteenth-century New York or Virginia. Occasionally married women ignored the legal restrictions of their *feme covert* status and engaged in economic activity.[27] Although their participation in the economy was minimal, it does at least point to the problem of relying on law codes to describe the experiences or the treatment of women. Legal codes by their very nature are proscriptive rather than descriptive. They establish the legal definitions of how property is conveyed, how family relationships are ordered, and how a society functions. They at once draw minimal boundaries, set guidelines, and specify procedures, but cannot fully capture the daily reality of individual men's or women's lives.

Women, Property, and Authority in Southside Virginia, 1735–1775

In the early decades of the eighteenth century increasing numbers of settlers began to migrate from the more settled tobacco counties along the eastern seaboard and penetrate the piedmont of Virginia. After 1730 the tide of settlement increased dramatically as colonial land policies became less restricted, and more and more pioneers poured into the area lying south of the James River and east of the Blue Ridge Mountains. As settlers and their families entered the Southside of Virginia, they established small farms, planted corn and later tobacco crops, and recreated the same legal and religious institutions they had known in the older settlements.[28]

In 1734 the settlers in the eastern section of the Southside began to complain of the distance to the county seat, and they petitioned the Assembly at Williamsburg for institutions of local government. In response, the Assembly divided sprawling Prince George County and formally created Amelia County in 1735. Within two decades Amelia's population had swelled to 7,000, and the small farmers and planters in the northernmost corner of the county petitioned the

Assembly for the creation of a new county. In 1754 the Assembly broke off the northwestern portion of Amelia and formally established Prince Edward County.[29] Within the next few years, a similar process of growth, expansion, and county-building occurred further south along the Virginia-North Carolina border. In 1765 the Assembly divided Lunenburg County and created Mecklenburg County.[30]

Part of Virginia's rapidly growing Southside, Amelia, Prince Edward, and Mecklenburg counties were not settled by the wealthy political elite of Virginia. Although men such as William Byrd II and Colonel Richard Randolph had economic interests in the area, they did not abandon their elegant and comfortable tidewater plantations and actually settle in the Southside. The settlers who cleared the land and who built houses and barns in the Southside comprised what one historian has characterized as the "anonymous hundreds."[31] Many were illiterate, most were relatively poor, and the society they built was rugged, often crude, and lacked the material comforts enjoyed by the aristocracy of Virginia.

In this rural, isolated landscape, with its dispersed farms and outlying plantations, what position did women occupy? What were the attitudes and realities that influenced their lives? Although much of the data is sketchy, certain broad outlines are apparent. As in other rural areas, women's lives followed daily routines of difficult and monotonous work. Typically, farm women and their daughters spent considerable time in household manufacture. Edmund S. Morgan notes that the Virginia farm woman had to "spin cotton, flax and wool, . . . look after the hogs and poultry, milk the cows, make butter and cheese, bake bread, clean the house, and get the meals, besides bearing and rearing children."[32] In addition, many Southside women had to work in the fields and help their husbands and fathers plant corn, weed and transplant tobacco, and harvest crops.[33] Essentially, women's primary sphere of activity centered around the home and family concerns. The manner books and morality tracts of the eighteenth century stressed that marriage was woman's "natural calling," and evidence from local court and church records indicates that most Southside women did marry and rear large families.[34]

The court records left by the settlers in the Southside shed important light on women's lives in the private sphere of the family. Unlike many Southern counties whose legal documents have been lost or destroyed, Amelia, Prince Edward, and Mecklenburg contain a complete run of court records. These legal documents, particularly the wills written in the years prior to the Revolution, offer valuable insights into the treatment of women in agricultural societies and women's access to property.

Property: Dower and the Southern Family

Virginia statutory law dictated the overall conveyance of property when a man died intestate. Based on common-law tradition, intestacy laws gave the eldest son the bulk of his father's real estate and an equal share of his personal property, which was divided among all the children, both male and female. The widow received one-third of the intestate's land and slaves as well as one-third of the personal property; at her death the real estate reverted to the couple's eldest son.[35]

Although Virginia intestacy laws clearly favored males, they alone do not accurately represent women's access to property.[36] A man could dispose of his economic assets as he saw fit by his last will and testament; the only legal limitation was that a husband was required to provide his wife with her minimum dower. An examination of the 394 wills probated in the three county courts of the Southside reveals that the testators diverged significantly from the inheritance patterns suggested by the laws regulating property distribution of intestates.[37] As the male testators disposed of the land, cattle, and slaves they had taken a lifetime to accumulate, their primary concern was that when possible, all members of the family, male and female, receive a share of the estate. The testators ignored primogeniture, tried to give all of their sons land, and proved generous in their treatment of the women in their families.

From 1735 to 1775 approximately one-fifth of the Southside fathers bequeathed land to their daughters, although colonial statutes governing the distribution of intestate real estate excluded daughters. In 1771 Upton Edmonson of Amelia County left his son and two daughters tracts of land. Benjamin received a 204-acre plantation in the county; Constant was bequeathed a 385-acre plantation in adjacent Mecklenburg, and Mary inherited her father's original dwelling plantation in Amelia. In 1751 William Watson demonstrated a similar generosity toward his daughter. He gave her a 2,650-acre tract along Bush River and left his son his house and 1,300 acres in Amelia. Such bequests were at the expense of the eldest sons and reflected the testators' desires that their daughter have an equitable share of their estates, probably to use as dowries or marriage portions.[38]

The men who gave their daughters land were usually among the elite in the Southside; it was only the wealthy who possessed enough economic resources to bequeath sufficient land to all members of the family.[39] As Amelia County became more settled during the course of the eighteenth century, however, the daughters of the wealthy began to receive fewer bequests of land. (See Table 1.)

During the first decade of settlement, 29 percent of the testators who had daughters bequeathed them land; in the decade just prior to the Revolution, this figure declined to 14 percent. It may be that the testators, facing a more populated county, began to perceive that the family resources could not sustain all of the sons and daughters, and still provide for the economic support of the widow. In this competition for family resources, it was daughters who received less land, although many continued to receive substantial legacies of slaves and personal property.

Wives and mothers, on the other hand, had significantly more access to both real and personal property. From 1735 to 1775, slightly more than 77 percent (N=185) of the testators in Amelia and Prince Edward assigned their wives more than traditional legal thirds. Further south, the Mecklenburg wills demonstrate a similar

TABLE   1

LAND DEVISE TO DAUGHTERS

Amelia County, 1735-75			
Year Will Written	N	N	%
1735-45	17	5	29%
1746-55	30	8	27%
1756-65	43	5	12%
1766-75	59	8	14%
Total:	149N	26N	17%
N=149			

SOURCE: Amelia County Will Books, 1:1734-71, 2:1771-80, 3:1780-86.

pattern—76 percent (N=28) of the men diverged from the legal code, and their widows acquired sizable portions of their estates.[40] (See Tables 2 and 3.)

Although the legacies varied, generally the wife tended to receive the dwelling house, land, and the balance of the husband's personal property, usually farm implements, furniture, household goods, and livestock. Particularly in Amelia just prior to the Revolution, if the family were wealthy enough to own slaves, the testator usually bequeathed his wife more slaves than the minimum "thirds" required by law. The legacy a man left his wife constituted the necessary equipment to run an agricultural operation in the eighteenth-century South, and he fully expected his spouse to use her legacy to support herself and their children.

This expectation was closely tied to and reinforced by certain demographic features of the Southside. The critical decision to leave a wife a substantial legacy, more than her dower, hinged on the age of the testator and the presence of minor children in the household. Although the Southside birth and death records have been lost or destroyed, the wills themselves provide important information about the demographic contours of the family which significantly influenced a widow's access to economic resources.

By applying techniques developed by Lois Carr, P. M. G. Harris, and Russell Menard for plotting life-cycles in colonial Maryland, and modified for the Southside, a pattern underlying the property bequests to wives emerges.[41] Whenever a man was elderly, he tended to give all of his property to his adult children and grandchildren and charge his eldest son with seeing that his mother had "gentle maintenance." Approximately sixteen of the testators in Amelia and Prince Edward were elderly when they wrote their wills, and of these, nine individuals gave their wives less than dower.[42]

At the other extreme of the life-cycle, men recently married and whose children were all very young tended to give their wives far more than their dower. Approximately fifty-six testators died within a few years of marrying, and either had not yet had children, or the children were very young. In 1775, for example, Branch Jones of Amelia County gave his wife his entire estate and then ordered that at her death or subsequent remarriage the property revert to the couple's only child, an infant daughter "born a few days before the making of this will."[43]

It appears that whenever a man had minor children, he tended to

TABLE 2

REQUESTS OF HUSBANDS TO WIVES
MECKLENBURG COUNTY
1735-75

N	All Estate		All Estate for Widowhood		Dwelling Plantation for Widowhood		Dwelling House for Widowhood		Dwelling Plantation for Life		Dwelling House for Life		More Than Dower in Other Form		Dower or Less or Unknown	
	N	%	N	%	N	%	N	%	N	%	N	%	N	%	N	%
238	23	10	19	8	43	18	5	2	65	27	3	1	27	11	53	22

SOURCE: Amelia County Will Books, 1:1734-71, 2:1771-80, 3:1780-86; Prince Edward County Will Book, 1:1754-85.

TABLE 3

REQUESTS OF HUSBANDS TO WIVES
MECKLENBURG COUNTY
1765-75

N	All Estate		All Estate for Widowhood		Dwelling Plantation Widowhood		More Than Dower in Other Form		Dower or Less or Unknown	
	N	%	N	%	N	%	N	%	N	%
37	5	14	6	16	7	19	10	27	9	24

SOURCE: Mecklenburg County Will Book, 1:1765-82.

give his wife more than her legal minimum. Many men in their middle years had young children living within the household as well as adult children who had already left home. Slightly more than 80 percent of these fathers bequeathed substantial legacies to their wives, often with the stipulation that they were to support themselves and their young children. In 1755 Daney Stanly wrote: "My Will is my loving Wife Edith Stanly shall have the use and profits of my whole Estate both real and personal until my Son John shall come to the age of twenty-one years. She giving my children Sufficient Maintenance."[44]

Although the Mecklenburg wills are even less detailed than those probated in Amelia and Prince Edward and do not reveal the testator's age, they still testify to the presence of minor children in the household. Sixty-two percent of the Mecklenburg testators who were survived by young children left their widows more than the minimum ordered by law.[45]

The wives of the more wealthy testators tended to receive legacies worth more than their poorer counterparts, but, wealthy or poor, testators' wives usually received more than their legal minimum of the estate whenever there were minor children. Generous property bequests to Southside daughters were tied more to class lines than were bequests to wives, and the testators' wives always received a far larger amount of the estate than did their daughters.

The age structure of the Southside family, however, did not always operate totally to the wife's economic advantage. The concern for minor children led many testators to restrict their wives' legacies. The Southside husbands did not usually give their wives land outright, or in fee simple; instead they usually bequeathed it to their spouses for their lifetimes or on the condition that the women remain unmarried. From 1735 to 1775 approximately half of the Southside testators restricted their wives' legacies. The most common restriction concerned their widows' remarriage; if a woman contracted a second marriage, the property would revert to the children of the first marriage. Such stipulations were not a negative reflection on the wife, but rather demonstrated a man's fear that the property he had originally set aside for both his widow and children might be wasted by a subsequent husband. By making legacies revert to the children, the testator at once secured his family's future while his widow remained single, and protected his children's legacies from a stepfather.[46]

Undoubtedly the age structure of the household had a major influence on women's access to economic resources. But feelings of affection did, too, although this is a factor less susceptible to measurement. In 1757 Samuel Cobbs, the court clerk of Amelia, gave his wife Edith all of his real estate in fee simple and most of his personal property. For emotional reasons he left his wife far more than her dower.

> As I have now almost finished my Will by which I have given a very extensive Power to my Wife, the inducement thereto and in gratitude to her I now mention. She has been my Wife near Forty Years during which Time hath always been Kind, loving and obedient to me without affection. My children are hers I commit them to her care. As my circumstances are now I could not provide for both and I do think it my Duty to provide for a Wife now in the Decline of life who so well Deserved it from me.[47]

Authority: Guardians and Executrixes

Most of the testators' widows received not only far more property than the legal code ordered but also significant amounts of authority and responsibility. The Southside widow was only rarely deprived of custody of her children, despite the fact that the legal code and books on childrearing at the time downplayed the idea of a mother having any impact on, or being competent to rear her children.[48] Less than 3 percent of the Amelia fathers named guardians for their children or overseers of their estates other than the mothers; only two Mecklenburg fathers deprived their wives of custody; and not one individual did so in Prince Edward.[49]

This decision to name the wife as guardian was not made because the father had no other male to turn to. Even during the earliest years of settlement, many men had male relatives living in the area or adult sons they could name as guardians of younger children. The decision to consign the minor children to their mother's care reflected a testator's belief in his wife's competency and responsibility. Occasionally the men specifically charged their wives with rearing the children in a "decent and Christian manner" or with making sure they received a year or two of schooling so that they could read the Bible. The majority of men, however, simply contented themselves with granting their wives total and complete authority to rear the children as they should think "fit and proper." Several fathers also bolstered their wives' authority over minor children by giving the women control over the pursestrings. In 1771 Elkanah Crenshaw of Amelia lent his wife his entire estate both real and personal. He indicated that his three sons would receive their inheritance only when their mother decided that the "Estate can afford it."[50]

The handful of men who deprived their wives of custody were men of wealth and were among the political and social elite in the Southside. Each owned extensive land, several slaves, and left personal estates in excess of £1000. These wealthy planters usually gave their children handsome legacies, often bequeathing them large plantations in different areas of Virginia. In such circumstances they tended to rely on other wealthy planters, often business acquaintances, to oversee the children's legacies and to serve as guardians. In 1765 James Hill asked Edmund Booker, a member of a prominent Amelia family, to rear his five minor children and oversee the tracts of land in Amelia and Lunenburg counties that he left in trust for his children. As a wealthy planter himself, Booker was probably more qualified to manage the children's plantations than was Hill's wife. In any case when Hill died in 1765, his children and their estates came under Booker's care.[51]

In keeping with their elevated social and economic position, the wealthy planters often desired that their children should receive specialized training and education. In 1770 John Scott deprived his wife of custody and asked four of his friends to serve as the guardians for his two young sons, John and Joseph, as well as executors of his estate, which was worth well over £1500. Scott asked his friends, all members of prominent families in Amelia, to "have my Sons well Educated and by them bound out to some person to learn them . . . at ministry or a profession."[52] Scott felt that his friends were better qualified in choosing individuals to educate his children than was his wife.

Scott and Hill were unusual in depriving their wives of child custody. Men of more moderate means than Scott and Hill had more limited expectations for their children's education and assumed that their spouses were perfectly competent to serve as guardians.

Widows in the Southside also received grants of authority from their spouses that enabled them to enter the legal and economic sectors of society, primarily as their spouses' executrixes. One of the most vital decisions a person made when writing a will was who to name as executor. Legally the executor was reponsible for paying the decedent's debts, carrying out personal requests, and dispensing the legacies. Slightly more than half of the Amelia testators appointed their wives to this important position; 78 percent of the Prince Edward husbands did so; and 57 percent of the Mecklenburg men named their wives.[53]

As Amelia County became more settled, however, the men began to rely less on their spouses. In the first decade of settlement, 65 percent (N=13) of the testators had appointed their wives, but by 1775 this percentage had declined to 43. In the years immediately before the Revolution, the men began to ask their eldest sons to administer their estates. This change may have been due to the maturation of the testators' sons. Traditionally settlement is undertaken by young men, either bachelors or men who had just begun their families. As the original settlers and their families matured, a large group of male children probably reached legal age and were thus able to serve as executors. As Amelia became more populated and as more elaborate kin networks were established, the farmers had less need to rely on their wives, although many continued to do so. Despite the increased reliance on eldest sons in the years just

TABLE 4

EXECUTORIAL APPOINTMENTS
AMELIA COUNTY, 1735-75

Year Will Written		Wives Named as Executors	
	N	N	%
1735-45	20	13	65%
1746-55	37	23	62%
1756-65	51	29	57%
1766-75	75	32	43%
TOTALS	183	97	53%
N=183			

SOURCE: Amelia County Will Books, 1:1734-71, 2:1771-80, 3:1780-86.

before the Revolution, throughout the county's colonial period a large proportion of men asked their wives to be their executrixes.

The Southside wife was not unique in serving as an executrix. In both the seventeenth and eighteenth centuries, colonial wives frequently served in this capacity. In fact, the custom was so widespread throughout colonial America that Benjamin Rush, a signer of the Declaration of Independence, argued that all women ought to receive far more education in mathematics and bookkeeping since they needed these skills as their husbands' executrixes.[54]

Ultimately a widow's access to property and authority within the family unit depended on the composition and age-structure of the nuclear family. The wills probated during the colonial period indicate that it was primarily in their roles as wives and mothers that women received land, slaves, and personal property as well as a measure of personal and legal authority.

Although the wills are useful in providing this type of information and in describing actual behavior, they are an incomplete source. Ultimately, the probate records just analyzed indicate male perceptions, male concerns, and male attitudes, and they tell us relatively little about how women acted or what they believed. These documents provide a snapshot of the Southside family, frozen at the moment a husband or father wrote his will. Perhaps more importantly for our purposes, is the exploration of women's responses to the social, economic, and legal changes that their spouses' deaths wrought.

The Widow as Feme Sole—Her New Status and Role

On September 9, 1766, Captain Obediah Woodson, planter and prominent citizen of Prince Edward County, Virginia, wrote his last will and testament. He commended his soul to God, consigned his body to the grave, and bequeathed all of his worldly goods to his wife and five children. Like many testators in eighteenth-century Virginia, Woodson tried to ensure that all of his sons and his widow would have enough to support themselves after his death. Obediah, David, and Jacob, his three oldest sons, each received a thousand acres in Bedford County as well as a smaller portion of land surrounding Woodson's plantation in Prince Edward County. Daniel, an underage son, was given a 400-acre tract in Prince Edward. The boys' mother, Constant, was left the house and the remaining acres in the original plantation. At her own death, the dwelling house and 150 acres were to revert to the couple's youngest son, Charles. While all five of his sons received adequate portions of land, Woodson also gave his wife a handsome legacy. Besides gaining the use of the house and the 150 acres for her life, she received all of his slaves and personal property outright.[55]

Within a few months of writing his will, Captain Woodson was dead. His death caused grief and a sense of loss and also set in motion a series of events that completely disrupted the life his family had known. The oldest boys probably left their parents' home, and with their father's legacy, began separate lives of their own. Obediah and Jacob each built separate dwellings in Prince Edward County, while David, apparently moved to Bedford County as least fifty miles away from his widowed mother. Constant, deprived of a husband and faced with the prospect of her three oldest sons leaving home, had to deal with practical, everyday difficulties as well as grief. Although she had thirteen slaves to work her portion of the land, and unlike some widows was not destitute, she had lost the four males in her immediate family who had overseen those slaves, decided what crops to plant, and managed the plantation. Now, besides attending to her regular domestic duties, she had to run the plantation alone and provide both for herself and her two very young children, Daniel and Charles.[56]

In an agricultural community the death of a married man had profound personal, economic, and social consequences for all his survivors. Older children who had previously postponed marriage, could now afford to wed, subsidized by their late father's legacy. Younger children, deprived of a father, beccame increasingly dependent on their widowed mother for economic support and parental guidance. The widow, especially if her late husband had appointed her as sole executrix, as Obediah Woodson had done, had to appear in court, settle his debts, and dispense his legacies, while she at the same time tried to support herself and her minor children.

Alexander Keyssar, in his pioneering study of widowhood in eighteenth-century Massachusetts, suggests that the colonial widow stood at the very center of all the changes caused by a married man's death.[57] The very fact of his death altered her life more than that of any other member of the nuclear family. Her legal status, her economic position, and her social standing within the community changed dramatically. Since her husband's death dissolved the

marriage bond, legally the widow was now a *feme sole*. She could
enter into contracts, sue her debtors, control her personal property,
manage her land, execute a will, or sign a deed. Economically, her
husband's death meant that the material resources of the family unit
had been reduced, and she now faced the prospect of a lower stan-
dard of living. Socially, much of the status she had derived from her
husband's position within the community ended with his death.
Widow Woodson no longer enjoyed the same measure of prestige
she had when her husband served as captain in the local militia or as
vestryman and churchwarden of St. Patrick's Parish.

Prior to Keyssar's work, historians had ignored how eighteenth-
century society dealt with the problem of widowhood or how the
widow herself coped with her new status and roles. This neglect
was not due to a scarcity of sources but rather to a reliance on a
few isolated literary sources which distorted the reality for most
eighteenth-century women in Virginia. For the most part, it was
assumed that widows remarried rapidly, and if necessary, frequently. Supposedly even elderly women remarried, their "share"
of their late husbands' estates giving them an edge in the marriage
market over younger but less wealthy women. Occasional, but col-
orful, marriage announcements in the *Virginia Gazette* seemed to
make the point clearly.

> Yesterday was married, in Henrico, Mr. William Carter third
> son of Mr. John Carter, aged twenty-three, to Mrs. Sarah
> Ellyson, Relict of Mr. Gerard Ellyson, deceased, aged eighty
> five, a sprightly old Tit, with three Thousand Pounds
> Fortune.[58]

If widowhood was indeed a temporary and easily rectified condition in the eighteenth century, neither society, the family, nor the
widow had to worry about the economic problems associated with
that state. Furthermore, given the restrictions imposed by coverture, if widows did not remain single for long, it would follow that
most Southside women rarely had significant access to property or
played a role within the colonial economy.[59] However, this was not
the case, as an examination of marriage bonds and ministers' returns
reveals.

Although parish records have not survived for the Southside,
the marriage bonds and ministers' returns can establish whether

"most" widows did or did not remarry. Virginia statutory law required that before the county clerk could grant the necessary marriage license to a couple, a third party had to post bond guaranteeing that both the bride and groom had reached their twenty-first birthday or had obtained their parents' consent to the prospective match. In an effort to prevent clandestine marriages, every minister in the colony was legally required to report any marriage ceremony he performed to the county clerk. It was in the best interests of both the clerk and the minister to adhere to the law and keep careful records. If they were derelict in their duties, they could be fined and/or imprisoned.[60]

The collected and published marriage bonds and ministers' returns for Amelia, Prince Edward, and Mecklenburg counties show that relatively few of the testators' widows in the Southside remarried. Less than 9 percent of these widows are known to have contracted a second marriage. In all three counties the percentage of widows entering upon a second marriage is far lower than traditional literary sources seem to suggest. Even allowing for some underregistration in the vital records, the 9 percent figure among this group of women is not high enough to warrant the conclusion that "most" widows remarried.[61]

Another source supplements this information. Virginia law required that most individuals who died within the colony have their estates inventoried and recorded at the local county court. Occasionally the inventory contains the name of the intestate's wife, usually when she served as the administratrix of the estate. These names can then be checked in the index to the marriage bonds and ministers' returns. Again, as in the case of the testators' widows, relatively few of these women remarried.[62]

Recent investigations of widowhood spurred by Keyssar's work, have made the important point that remarriage rates reflect a tangled component of need, opportunity, and desire.[63] Many Southside widows of either testators or intestates did not economically need to contract a second marriage. With the work provided by either her slaves or her minor children, the widow did not need the labor of a new spouse to help her exploit either her dower rights or her sizable legacy. In addition, since many of the testator's widows lost some of their wealth upon remarriage, it was not to their economic advantage to contract a second marriage unless their prospective spouses' wealth offset the loss. Of course, a widow who wished to remarry could exercise her legal option, renounce her first husband's legacy and the attendant restrictions, if any, and receive a portion of the personal property outright and a life interest in one-third of the lands and slaves. A few women who remarried exercised this legal option, but it was a rare occurrence. Even if a widow renounced her original legacy, she lost control of her property upon her second marriage. A widow as a *feme sole* could enter into a contract with a prospective spouse and protect her wealth by an antenuptial agreement, but again this was a very rare occurrence in the Southside.

Recent studies suggest that the widow's age may be the most reliable predictor of the remarriage rate.[64] Analyses of remarriage in populations where birth and death registers are complete suggest that only widows who were relatively young contracted second marriages. Widows who were older or who were at least old enough to have adult children tended not to remarry. Even though it is impossible to determine the ages of the Southside widows in most cases, evidence suggests that a woman's place in the life-cycle influenced the low remarriage rate. Many testators' widows had both adult and minor children at the time of their spouses' deaths. Moreover, court records indicate that few widows survived their spouses for several decades. The average duration of widowhood was approximately ten years, the median, six years. Women in their middle years with some economic resources may have felt they had enough to support themselves and any minor children until the children reach adulthood. In addition, younger women in the population may have been more attractive marital prospects. Whether the widow chose not to remarry or whether she did not have the opportunity, the fact remains that most Southside widows did not contract second marriages.

The primary economic activity of the testator's widow usually involved running her late husband's farm or plantation in addition to performing her traditional domestic duties. Over 65 percent (N=180) of the testator's widows received control over real estate. Undoubtedly widows pursued many of the same tasks they had while their spouses were alive. And it may be that their legacy reflected the fact that their spouses knew the women were familiar with the agricultural operation. Southside legal records contain several instances of widows coming to court to register cattle marks or determine the age of slaves, which are examples of their new responsibilities associated with maintaining a farm or plantation in the eighteenth-century South.

Apparently, the widow assumed most of these responsibilities herself and did not rely on an adult son or male friend of her late husband. In 1757 Sarah Bine petitioned the Amelia Court for permission to alter the route of the public road running through her plantation. The Court agreed to appoint a commission to investigate the matter. Shortly thereafter Sarah met with the commissioners, explained why the present road was a great "inconvenience" and proposed an alternative route. Sarah was evidently persuasive. A few months later the commissioners reported to the Court, and the justices granted Sarah permission to alter the public road, noting that the changes she proposed would be more convenient both for herself and the general public.[65]

The 1767 tithable or tax lists of Amelia County provide additional evidence that many women assumed sole responsibility for operating their farms and did not rely on their adult children. According to Virginia law, taxes were levied on every slave over sixteen years of age and on every white male over sixteen. The 1767 document is unusual in listing the number of tithables in each household and also the number of acres held by the landowners. Several widows are listed as heads of families, and the data indicate that many of these women cultivated farms or ran plantations alone. Slightly more than two-thirds of these women lived in homes without adult, male children. These widows directed their slaves to build fences and barns, plant corn or tobacco, and oversaw their work in the house and the fields. Ann Hill, for example, operated a 360-acre tract with the labor of seven adult slaves. No adult children or male overseer lived with her, and she assumed total responsibility over her late husband's agricultural operation.[66]

The 1767 tax list also throws additional light on the widow's participation in the agricultural sector. A few widows evidently received slaves but no land from their late husbands. In such circumstances, the widow probably supported herself and her minor children by leasing these slaves to her neighbors. Mrs. Anne Tanner, for example, had six slaves but did not cultivate any land. She most likely rented some of these slaves and their labor to neighboring planters or small farmers during periods of high labor demand or for the whole year.[67]

Besides managing plantations and small farms or deriving an income by leasing slaves, a few Southside widows also ran mills. Eleven men had assigned rights to their milling operations by their

last wills and testaments; the widow frequently received total authority over and sole reponsibility for operating her late husband's
mill.[68] In 1759, for example, Abraham Cocke of Amelia County,
gave his wife sole authority over the mill he owned on Little Notto-
way Creek. Mary Cocke, the mother of five minor children, ran the
mill and managed the dwelling plantation for several years. At her
death, the mill reverted to an eldest son, Abraham, while her personal property and slaves descended to her younger sons.[69] Similarly, Joseph Scott, of Amelia County, left his wife the mill, his
plantations, and several slaves. Sarah Scott exercised total control
over both the mill and the land until her youngest son, John,
reached legal age.[70]

    As millers, these widows were legally responsible for keeping the
mill in working order, seeing that necessary repairs were effected,
and providing accurate weights and measures. In return for these
services, and in lieu of a fee, the widow received a percentage of the
grain she ground for an individual, usually one-eighth of the total.[71]
The widow who operated a mill was in a fortunate economic position. She could secure enough grain for her family's consumption
without planting, growing, or tending a wheat or corn crop. Or she
could supplement the family income by growing grain on the land
left her by her late husband, sell the crop and still have enough
grain for home consumption because of her milling operation.

    Although most women ran their late husbands' mills alone, a few
oversaw its operation in conjuction with an adult son. In 1759, for
example, Henry Ligon, Sr., of Prince Edward County, gave his wife
and his older son, William, a half interest each in his mill and
divided his dwelling plantation between them. Sarah Ligon used her
interest in the mill, her land, and the labor of four slaves to support
herself and to rear two minor daughters. When she herself died in
1785, her interest in the mill reverted to her son, William.[72]

    Although most widows supported themselves by engaging in
solely agricultural enterprises, such as farming or milling, occasionally an unusual woman became involved in other types of economic
activities. Constant Woodson, widow of Captain Obediah Woodson
of Prince Edward County, was such a woman. While her husband
was still alive, Constant had been active within the county in caring
for the sick. Like most women on isolated farms and outlying plantations, she had gained some basic medical experience caring for the
sick members of her own family and overseeings ailing slaves. Be-

cause there were few, if any, physicians living in the county, Constant Woodson, like other plantation wives, was probably called on by her neighbors to set broken bones, deliver babies, and make concoctions for colds and fevers. After her husband's death, she parlayed her medical experience into a lucrative and profitable profession.[73]

About the time her husband died, Constant notified the House of Burgesses in Williamsburg that she had discovered a cure for cancer. She offered to publish her formula in return for a "Valuable consideration." The Burgesses agreed to pay her £100 if a committee of reputable physicians would certify that her treatments were successful. Although there is no record of whether she ever received the money, her petition attracted public notice and she continued treating cancer patients in Prince Edward and throughout the colony for a fee.[74]

Although Constant Woodson was financially secure, because of her "profession" as well as her late husband's legacy, widowhood for some was a time of serious economic deprivation. If a family did not own land or was very poor, the death of the husband and the loss of his labor, meant that his widow would have a difficult time eking out even a marginal existence. When her older children were too poor to help her or when she was solely responsible for young, dependent children, a widow had to rely on the local parish for aid.

The vestry records for many Southside parishes have not survived, but the parish records for Prince Edward County indicate that a few indigent widows received some help from this institution. From 1755 to 1774, approximately twenty women appeared on the parish relief roll; most of them widows. Although the vestry recognized its obligation to provide for indigent women, the family still retained the primary responsibility for caring for its members. Rather than paying a widow directly or providing her with separate housing, the vestry reimbursed her adult children. In 1770, for example, Benjamin Johns received £7.0.0 for "supporting his mother." From 1770 to 1774 the vestry gave Johns, evidently in economic difficulty himself, a total of £30 to help him maintain and care for his widowed mother.[75]

A few indigent widows were able to supplement their economic resources by serving in salaried church positions. In 1757 Judith Rutledge succeeded her husband, Richard, as the sexton of the Sandy River Church in Prince Edward County. She was responsible for cleaning the church, escorting the parishioners to their pews each Sunday, opening the church prior to any services, closing it after the congregation left, washing the minister's surplice and altar linen as well as laying out the dead for burial. Judith served as the sexton of the Sandy River Church for almost twenty years. Her salary, paid by the vestry, was the same as her late husband's when he had occupied this position, 312 pounds of tobacco annually. Similarly, Mrs. Mary Barnett served as the sexton of another Anglican congregation in Prince Edward County. Named as the sexton of Frenches Church in 1771, Mary Barnett performed the same type of duties as Judith Rutledge and received a comparable salary.[76]

The Anglican congregations in Prince Edward County were not unusual or unique in having their female widowed parishioners participate in church affairs. Widows in several Southside parishes assumed minor jobs related to the administration of various church affairs. The Bristol Parish Vestry (one of the original Anglican parishes in the Southside) named Susanna Woodlief as sexton, and prior to 1720 appointed Elizabeth Kennon to operate a ferry to bring parishioners to church. Elizabeth, probably either a widow or an indigent spinster, received twenty-five hundred pounds of tobacco annually for performing this service and occupied the post for at least fifteen years.[77]

Hiring women, usually widows, for church positions was a shrewd and realistic response by local churches to the economic hardships that widowhood might entail. By appointing Judith Rutledge as sexton when her husband died and vacated the post, the vestry in Prince Edward gained the services of someone marginally familiar with the duties of the position and, at the same time, reduced the possibility that Widow Rutledge would become a candidate for the parish relief rolls.

The court records of the Southside imply that, as their late husbands' executrixes, many women took their positions seriously and performed their duties with a high degree of competence. In 1757 Edith Cobbs, executrix and widow of Samuel Cobbs, the court clerk of Amelia County, discovered that her husband had neglected to record several legal documents such as land sales, inventories, and estate accounts at the courthouse. Within a few weeks of his death, she notified the court of her late husband's "oversight" and asked that the justices "would undertake to indulge her so far as to order and direct that Benjamin Harris" assist her in compiling these important documents and entering them in the court records. The justices "indulged" Widow Cobbs and even granted her additional time a few months later when the lengthy task was not yet completed. Eventually Edith Cobbs finished sorting through her husband's personal papers, extracting the necessary legal documents, and the Amelia court records were brought up to date.[78]

As her husband's executrix, Edith Cobbs was not only responsible for seeing that his official duties were completed, but in concluding his economic affairs as well. From 1757 to the time of her own death in 1761, she appeared in court several times to collect debts due to either her late husband's estate or to herself directly. She was successful in collecting several of those debts and in preserving the estate for the eventual use of her two minor children, Samuel and John, and her two married daughters, Theodosia and Judith. When she herself died in 1761, her children received sizable tracts of land and divided their mother's personal property, which was worth over £1500.[79]

As her husband's executrix, Edith Cobbs, like many widows in Southside Virginia, exercised considerable control over the economic resources of the family unit. Edmund S. Morgan, in his social history of seventeenth-century Virginia, found that when a widow served as an executrix she frequently delayed paying the other heirs their legacies and enjoyed the wealth of her late husband's estate for a considerable period of time.[80] It is impossible to determine whether this was a common or widespread practice for the Southside widows during the eighteenth century. However, a few wills, left by the widows themselves, reveal that some women did occasionally delay paying the other heirs, usually the couple's children.

In 1759 John Wallace, Sr., of Amelia County, appointed his wife Mary as his sole executrix and ordered that as his children came of age they were to receive their share of his estate. When Mary Wallace died twenty-five years later, she had given some of her married sons and daughters their portions but had delayed paying three married daughters their legacies. Jane, Sally, and Molly had attained their legal majority some time previously, but contrary to their father's wishes, they had not received their inheritances. Such delays could reflect a desire to maintain parental authority or an effort to prevent family wealth from going outside the family to sons-in-law. In Mary Wallace's case, however, the delay probably reflected her desire to maintain control of a portion of the family wealth. In her will she made no effort to create separate estates for two of her married daughters and assigned one daughter's portion directly to her son-in-law and named him as the executor of her estate. Whatever her specific motivation, Mary Wallace kept control of a portion of her late husband's estate for several years longer than he had originally stipulated and only relinquished that control at the time of her own death in 1780.[81]

If Mary Wallace had not left a will, the only information about her would have been derived from her husband's will. Her own will expresses yet more about her life—that she delayed paying some of her children their legacies, that she did not remarry, and that her widowhood lasted for twenty-five years. The thirty-two wills left by Southside widows not only provide this type of information but also hint at gender differences. For example, in the 394 wills probated in the Southside courts the only bequest to charity was made by a woman. Francis Stokes of Amelia County ordered that her executors were to ensure that the "Poor of Raleigh Parish" received £25 from her estate.[82] Furthermore, women frequently made bequests to female friends and sisters, hinting at the importance of other women in their lives. In 1766 Judith Frank wrote: "I Give and bequeath all my Estate both Real and personal and Cash unto my Friend Mary Finney and to her heirs forever." Judith Frank also requested that her friend serve as the executrix of her estate.[83] Both Dorothy Crowder and Mary Gray left their estates to their sisters and appointed them as executrixes.[84] Oftentimes, such bequests and appointments were made at the expense of male relatives. Widows also turned to other women when they were worried about their young children. Judith Booker directed by her last will that her young daughter, Judith, "live with and under the care and Tuition of Mrs. [Edith] Cobbs."[85]

Taken together, the wills written by both men and women, as well as local church and court records, suggest the outlines of economic and legal realities—greater access to economic resources, some autonomy in the private sphere regarding decision-making and childrearing, and hint at slightly different value systems for female testators.

Widowhood entailed new duties and greater responsibilities for many women. As planters, farmers, sextons, and executrixes these widows possessed greater economic, religious, and legal responsibilities than they had while they were married, and they participated more fully in eighteenth-century society than sources emphasizing feminine dependency and subordination fully suggest.

Conclusion

A case study approach, focusing on the analysis of tax and probate records, undermines the traditional, highly restrictive view of Southern women. Although women in the Southside did not share the locus of power and authority exercised by wealthy white males, their position in the private sphere of the family was not as limited or limiting as proscriptive sources indicate. Men, by their last wills and testaments, often transferred the twin hallmarks of patriarchy, authority and property, to their wives.

The data from probate records suggest that a woman's place as daughter, wife, or widow profoundly influenced her access to property and authority. Some daughters of wealthy settlers received bequests of land from their fathers. However, this was not a widespread practice and declined during the period. Wives, on the other hand, were typically the beneficiaries of legacies from their husbands—legacies which generally reflected men's concern for their young children's welfare—and the practice continued as the Southside became more populated. Furthermore, few Southside widows remarried, and as widows, participated in significant economic and legal affairs, closely tied to familial concerns and responsibilities.

The diversity of probate records, the different treatment accorded wives and daughters, the different behavior of widows and wives, all call into question the theory of a "golden age" for women in the colonial period, as well as the notion of complete female limitation in a grim patriarchal milieu. Both views are oversimplified and neither adequately explains a complicated reality. Perhaps the entire debate about declining or improving status for women from the colonial to the national period is premature until the details of women's experiences and lifestyles are more fully reclaimed.

REFERENCES

I would like to thank Michael L. Nicholls and Lois Carr for reading and commenting on this research in various stages and for generously sharing their expertise.

In addition some of this material was presented as a paper at the Fifth Berkshire Conference on Women's History, 1981. The comments of Marylynn Salmon and Jessica Kross Ehrlich proved particularly helpful.

Whenever material from the Southside court and vestry records was quoted, the original spellings, capitalizations, and punctuations were retained. Similarly, the exact dates—month, day, and year—that appeared in the manuscript records were retained.

1. The earlier important works done on colonial women include Mary S. Benson, *Women in Eighteenth-Century America: A Study of Opinion and Usage* (New York, 1935); Richard B. Morris, *Studies in the History of American Law*, 2d ed. (New York, 1963, originally published in 1938), chaps. 2 and 3; Julia Cherry Spruill, *Women's Life and Work in the Southern colonies* (New York, 1972, originally published in 1938). For more recent analyses see fn. 2 below and Linda Kerber, *Women of the Republic: Intellect and Ideology in Revolutionary America* (Chapel Hill, 1980); Lyle Koehler, *A Search for Power: The "Weaker Sex" in Seventeenth-Century New England* (Urbana, 1980); Mary Beth Norton, *Liberty's Daughters: The Revolutionary Experience of American Women, 1750–1800* (Boston, 1980); Roger Thompson, *Women in Stuart England and America: A Comparative Study* (London, 1974).

2. Lois Green Carr and Lorena S. Walsh, "The Planter's Wife: The Experience of White Women in Seventeenth-Century Maryland" *William and Mary Quarterly*, 3d ser., no. 4, 34 (1977): 42–71; Marylynn Salmon, "Equality or Submersion? Feme Covert Status in Early Pennsylvania," in *Women of America: A History*, ed. Carol Ruth Berkin and Mary Beth Norton (Boston, 1979), pp. 92–111; Joan R. Gunderson and Gwen W. Gampel, "Married Women's Legal Status in Eighteenth-Century Virginia and New York," *William and Mary Quarterly*, 3d ser., no. 1 (1981): 114–34; Joan Hoff Wilson, "Hidden Riches: Legal Records and Women, 1750–1825," in *Woman's Being, Woman's Place: Female Identity and Vocation in American History*, ed. Mary Kelley, (Boston, 1979); idem "The Illusion of Change: Women and the American Revolution," in *The American Revolution: Explorations in the History of American Radicalism*, ed. Alfred F. Young, (Dekalb, Illinois, 1976), pp. 383–445.

3. For a discussion of colonial literacy see Kenneth A. Lockridge, *Literacy in Colonial New England: An Enquiry into the Social Context of Literacy in the Early Modern West* (New York, 1974), p. 92; Linda Auwers Bissel, "The Social Meaning of Female Literacy, Windsor, Connecticut, 1660–1775" (paper presented at Newberry Library Conference on Quantitative and Social Science Approaches in Early American History, Chicago, Ill., 6–8 October 1977). Because this study has concentrated on women's access to property during the eighteenth century, black women have not been included in the analysis.

4. Herbert G. Gutman, *The Black Family in Slavery and Freedom, 1750–1925* (New York, 1977).

5. James K. Somerville, "The Salem Woman in the Home, 1660–1770," *Eighteenth Century Life* I (1974):11.

6. Cited in Helena Mast Robinson, "The Status of the Feme Covert in Eighteenth Century Virginia" (M.A. thesis, University of Virginia, 1971), p. 3.

7. An excellent discussion of the proscriptive literature is contained in Spruill, *Women's Life and Work*, pp. 208–31.

8. Robinson, "Status of Feme Covert," pp. 7–11; Spruill, *Women's Life and Work,* chap. 16. For discussions of the extent to which the North American colonists transplanted English law see George Athan Billias, ed., *Law and Authority in Colonial American* (New York, 1970); Clara Ann Bowler, "Cartered Whores and White Shrouded Apologies: Slander in the County Courts of Seventeenth-Century Virginia," *Virginia Magazine of History and Biography* 85 (1977):11–26; David H. Fla-

herty, ed., *Essays in the History of Early American Law* (Chapel Hill, 1969);
Lawrence M. Friedman, *A History of American Law* (New York, 1973), pp. 13–90;
Gunderson and Gampel, "Married Women's Legal Status," pp. 114–34; C. Ray
Keim, "Primogeniture and Entail in Colonial Virginia," *William and Mary Quarterly,*
3d ser., no. 4, 25 (1968):545–86; Morris, *Studies in the History of American Law,*
chaps. I and III; Patricia Ann Padgett, "Legal Status of Women in Colonial Virginia,
1700–1785" (M.A. thesis, College of William and Mary, 1967).

    9. St. George Tucker, ed., *Blackstone's Commentaries: with Notes of Reference,
To the Constitution and Laws of the Federal Government of the United States; and of
the Commonwealth of Virginia,* 5 vols. (Philadelphia, 1803), bk. 2, p. 129, fn. 12.
Although Tucker is primarily concerned with the corpus of Virginia state law that is
based on English precedent, he often notes colonial laws that were also based on
English common law. Also see Morris, *Studies in the History of American Law,* pp.
128–30.

    10. William Waller Hening, ed., *The Statutes at Large: Being a Collection of all
the Laws of Virginia, from the first Session of the Legislature in the Year 1619,* 13 vols.
(Richmond and Philadelphia, 1809–1823), 3:317, 4:223.

    11. Mary R. Beard, *Women As Force in History: A Study in Tradition and Reali-
ties* (New York, 1946), pp. 122–44.

    12. Salmon, "Equality or Submersion," pp. 98–101, 108–111.

    13. Amelia County Will Book 2, 1771–80 (microfilm, Virginia State Library,
Richmond, Virginia), p. 81.

    14. Hening, ed., *Statutes,* 5:410–11.

    15. Frederick Pollock and Frederic William Maitland, *The History of English
Law: Before the Time of Edward I,* 2 vols. (Cambridge, 1952, originally published in
1895), 2:424.

    16. Hening, *Statutes,* 2:212, 3:371–75, 5:444–48. For a perceptive discussion of
dower see Marylynn Salmon, "The Inheritance Rights of American Women, 1750–
1820: A Comparative Perspective," in *Women and the Law: A Social-Historical
Perspective,* ed. Kelly Weisberg (Cambridge, 1982). I would like to thank Dr. Salmon
for sending me her manuscript copy of this forthcoming article.

    17. Ibid., 5:410–11, 447.

    18. George Webb, *The Office and Authority of a Justice of the Peace* (Williams-
burg, 1736), p. 151.

    19. Tucker, ed., *Blackstone's Commentaries,* 1, 444–45.

    20. Spruill, *Women's Life and Work,* p. 343.

    21. Hening, ed., *Statutes,* 5:449; Tucker, ed., *Blackstone's Commentaries,* 1, 438,
452, 462.

    22. Spruill, *Women's Life and Work,* p. 345.

    23. Ibid., p. 335.

    24. Tucker, ed., *Blackstone's Commentaries,* 1, 439–41.

    25. Spruill, *Women's Life and Work,* p. 344.

    26. Hening, ed., *Statutes,* 3:172.

    27. Gunderson and Gampel, "Married Women's Legal Status," pp. 114–34.

    28. For the most complete analysis of Southside society see Michael L. Nicholls,
"Origins of the Virginia Southside, 1703–1753: A Social and Economic Study" (Ph.D
diss., College of William and Mary, 1972).

    29. Hening, ed., *Statutes,* 4:467–68, 6:379–80. No records accurately and com-
pletely indicate population size of any eighteenth-century Virginia county prior to the
Federal Census of 1790. Virginia historians usually estimate colonial population size
and growth by using a county's tithable or tax list. According to Virginia law, taxes
were levied on every black slave and white male over sixteen. According to the

formula suggested by Governor Robert Dinwiddie in 1756, white tithables are multi-plied by 4, black tithables by 2, and the totals are added together to estimate the size of the population. Robert Dinwiddie, *The Official Records of Robert Dinwiddie, Lieutenant Governor of the Colony of Virginia, 1751–1758*, 2 vols., ed. R. A. Brock (Richmond, 1883–1884), 2:353. The difficulties in using tithable records are de-scribed in detail in Edmund S. Morgan, *American Slavery American Freedom: The Ordeal of Colonial Virginia* (New York, 1975), pp. 395–442. For Amelia County's tithable figures see Nicholls, "Origins of the Virginia Southside," pp. 46, 120–22.

30. Hening, ed., *Statutes*, 8:41–42.

31. Nicholls, "Origins of the Virginia Southside," p. 17.

32. Edmund S. Morgan, *Virginians at Home: Family Life in the Eighteenth Cen-tury* (Charlottesville, 1963, originally published in 1952), p. 41. Virginia law required that almost every individual who died within the colony have his or her estate inven-toried and recorded at the local county court. The inventories list the amount and type of personal property. Agricultural tools and household equipment such as pots, pans, cards, and spinning wheels appear frequently.

33. Even by 1749, 54 percent of the resident, white male taxpayers in Amelia had no other source of labor within their household except themselves and possibly their wives. See Nicholls, "Origins of the Virginia Southside," p. 86.

34. Although the Southside marriage, birth, and death records have not survived, important demographic data may be derived from local probate records. Wills, for example, indicate that Southside families of six children were common. See fn. 41 below.

35. Hening, ed., *Statutes*, 5:444–48.

36. See Gunderson and Gampel, "Married Women's Legal Status," pp. 114–34.

37. For other studies which indicate that testators diverged from inheritance pat-terns suggested by laws regulating intestate property distribution see Keim, "Primo-geniture and Entail in Colonial Virginia"; Daniel Blake Smith, "Family Experience and Kinship in Eighteenth-Century Chesapeake Society" (Ph.D. diss. University of Virginia, 1977); James W. Deen, Jr., "Patterns of Testation: Four Tidewater Counties in Colonial America," *American Journal of Legal History* 16 (1972):154–75.

38. ACWB2, pp. 9–11; ACWB1, fol. 79.

39. For example, in 1750, Edward Booker, Sr., of Amelia County left his son the Winterham plantation and bequeathed the plantation on Saylow Creek to his daughter. In addition to these properties, Booker left a personal estate appraised at over £1200.

40. Unless otherwise noted, the quantitative data presented here are derived from material contained in Amelia County Will Books, 1:1734–71, 2:1771–80, 3:1780–86 (hereafter cited as ACWB); Prince Edward County Will Book 1:1754–85 (hereafter cited as PECWB); Mecklenburg County Will Book 1:1765–1782 (micro-film, Virginia State Library, Richmond, Virginia). Although all the wills considered in this analysis were written prior to 1776, some were not recorded in court until the testator died, often in the 1780s. All the wills recorded from 1735 to 1786 were examined in order to abstract those written during the colonial era. Of the 394 wills written prior to the Revolution, 275 were left by husbands whose wives were then living; 49 wills were left by bachelors; 38 wills were left by widowers; and 32 wills were left by women.

41. A study of Maryland inventories, "Social Stratification in Maryland, 1658–1705," being conducted by P. M. G. Harris, Russell Menard, and Lois Green Carr, under the auspices of the St. Mary's City Commission and with funds from the National Science Foundation (GS-32272). For an example of how this method can be used to plot life-cycles see Lorena S. Walsh, "Till Death Us Do Part: Marriage and

Family in Seventeenth-Century Maryland," in *The Chesapeake in the Seventeeth Century: Essays on Anglo-American Society,* ed. Thad W. Tate and David L. Ammerman (Chapel Hill, 1979), pp. 126–52.

42. For example, Gower Parkham of Amelia County gave his four adult children all of his estate, leaving no property to his wife, Archer. He charged his son James to use his legacy to support and care for his mother. See ACWB2, p. 359.

43. ACWB2, p. 144.

44. ACWB1, p. 126.

45. Approximately twenty-one of the Mecklenburg testators were survived by a wife and had minor children. Of this group, thirteen of these individuals gave their wives more than their dower.

46. In 1759 Isaac Robinson gave his wife the dwelling house, 100 acres of his land, and all of his personal property. He qualified his bequest by noting "in case my sd. Wife should Marry she then shall have but her thirds of my sd. hundred Acres of Land and moveables." At his wife's death or remarriage, the property reverted to the couple's youngest son Zachariah. See PECWB1, p. 86.

47. ACWB1, foll. 127–28.

48. Blackstone, when explaining the legal authority a man had over his children, dismissed the mother's possible influence or role because "she generally wants ability." See Tucker, ed., *Blackstone's Commentaries,* 1, 447.

49. Virginia law also permitted children to come into court and name their own guardian when their father died. The legal system of the colony tended to supervise "orphans' " upbringing and ensure that their estates were not wasted. Mothers might lose custody if they contracted a second marriage, and the court was concerned that the children's stepfather might waste the children's inheritance. Overall, the justices rarely removed the children from their mother's care when the testator named her as guardian.

50. ACWB2, pp. 28–29.

51. ACWB1, pp. 91–93.

52. ACWB2, pp. 46–48.

53. Hening, ed., *Statutes,* 5:454–67. Although there were 193 testators with wives in Amelia, 10 men failed to name executors, and therefore were not included in the data base. Of the 183 individuals who named executors, 97 men asked their wives to serve. In Prince Edward, 35 men named their wives and 21 Mecklenburg husbands did so.

54. Benjamin Rush, *Essays Literary, Moral and Philosophical* (Philadelphia, 1789), 75–77.

55. PECWB1, pp. 94–95.

56. Although it is impossible to determine the exact age of the children, information extracted from several sources indicates that when Obediah died in 1767, his two sons, Daniel and Charles, were very young. Constant's will, six years later, contains educational provisions for the two boys. Charles, apparently, was very young at the time of his father's death. When Obediah, his oldest brother, wrote his own will in 1776, he noted that Charles was still a minor. See PECWB1, pp. 160, 199–200. A variety of sources were used to determine the likelihood of the oldest boys leaving home at the time of their father's death. David disappears from the extant county and parish records about this time. There is no record of his serving on the grand jury, marrying within the county, or holding any church position. Apparently he moved to Bedford County. Both Obediah and Jacob remained in Prince Edward and built homes for themselves on their father's subdivided plantation. Obediah left his house to his brother Daniel in his will of 1776, and Jacob, by this time, had married and was the father of at least one son. Very likely each of these two sons (Obediah

and Jacob) had built their own residences about the time of their father's death. A state census of 1785 lists three separate dwellings for Jacob, Daniel, and Charles. Charles had inherited his father's original house, Daniel had inherited the house his brother Obediah had built and Jacob also had his own dwelling. See U.S., Bureau of the Census, *Heads of Families: At the First Census of the United States Taken in 1790, Records of the State Enumerations, 1782–1785* (Washington, D.C., 1908), p. 100.

57. Alexander Keyssar, "Widowhood in Eighteenth Century Massachusett: A Problem in the History of the Family," *Perspectives in American History*, 8 (1974):83.

58. Cited in Spruill, *Women's Life and Work*, p. 161.

59. Ibid., pp. 155, 366; Linda Grant De Pauw, "Land of the Unfree: Legal Limitations on Liberty in Pre-Revolutionary America," *Maryland Historical Magazine*, 68 (1973):355–68.

60. Hening, ed., *Statutes*, 3:441–44; 6:81–85.

61. Kathleen Booth Williams, ed., *Marriages of Amelia County, Virginia, 1735–1815* (Alexandria, Virginia, 1961), pp. 1–165; Catherine Lindsay Knorr, ed., *Marriage Bonds and Ministers' Returns of Prince Edward County, Virginia, 1754–1810.* (Virginia, 1950), pp. 1–109; Katherine Blackwell Elliott, ed., *Marriage Records 1765–1810, Mecklenburg County, Virginia* (South Hill, Virginia, 1963), pp. 1–185; Lois J. Kelley, "The Reality of Widowhood: Opportunities for Power and Authority in Mecklenburg County, Virginia, 1765–1782," seminar paper, History Department, Utah State University, Logan, Utah, 1980. Keyssar found that in eighteenth-century Massachusetts only 10 percent of the sixty widows he traced through the extant public records contracted a second marriage.

62. Hening, ed., *Statutes*, 5:462. The estate inventories and appraisals are contained in the Will Books of the three counties.

63. Susan Grigg, "Toward a Theory of Remarriage: Early Newburyport," *Journal of Interdisciplinary History*, 8 (1977):183–220.

64. Ibid.

65. Amelia County Order Book 5, 1757–60 (microfilm, Virginia State Library, Richmond, Virginia), pp. 38, 45. Hereafter cited as ACOB5.

66. I am grateful to Carol N. Funk, a graduate student in History at Utah State University, for providing me with this information. Of thirty-four women listed as heads of households, twenty-three lived in households without adult male children.

67. Ibid.

68. In five cases the widow received total and sole authority over her late husband's mill; in two cases she shared authority with an adult son; in three cases either the executors or children were responsible for the mill. In one case it is not clear whether or not the widow received any rights to her husband's mill.

69. ACWB1, pp. 169–72.

70. Ibid., fol. 56.

71. Hening, ed., *Statutes*, 6:556–60.

72. PECWB1, pp. 52–53, 352–53.

73. Herbert Clarence Bradshaw, *History of Prince Edward County, Virginia: From its Earliest Settlements Through its Establishment in 1754 to its Bicentennial Year* (Richmond, Virginia, 1954), p. 46.

74. John Pendleton Kennedy and Henry R. McIlwaine, eds., *Journal of the House of Burgesses of Virginia*, 13 vols. (Richmond, 1905–1915), 11:42, 124–25.

75. The Vestry Book of St. Patrick's Parish, pp. 35, 37, 39, 42, 46.

76. Ibid., pp. 7, 37.

77. Spruill, *Women's Life and Work*, pp. 304–303.

78. ACOB5, pp. 6, 42, 46.

79. Ibid., pp. 18, 25, 72; ACWB1, foll. 127–28, 200–201.

80. Morgan, *American Slavery American Freedon*, p. 166.

81. ACWB1, fol. 110; ACWB2, p. 360.
82. ACWB1, fol. 97.
83. ACWB1, p. 351.
84. ACWB1, p. 179; ACWB2, pp. 317–18.
85. ACWB1, fol. 70.

THE THRALL DIVORCE CASE:
A FAMILY CRISIS
IN EIGHTEENTH-CENTURY
CONNECTICUT

Alison Duncan Hirsch

On May 12, 1732, Hannah Thrall of Windsor, Connecticut, left her husband.[1] She and William were first cousins, had both lived in Windsor all their lives, and had been married for three and a half years.[2] Hannah said afterward that she only intended to leave for a short time, just until William's temper cooled, for they had quarreled several times and he had struck her. He denied that they had fought and claimed that she left only because she resented living with her mother-in-law. According to him, she never showed any intention of returning. When William sued for divorce in August 1735, he accused Hannah of adultery as well as desertion, although he did not specify with whom. Either accusation was sufficient grounds for divorce under the Connecticut law of 1667, which empowered the Court of Assistants to grant divorces on the grounds of "adultery, fraudulent contract, or willfull desertion for three years, with total neglect of duty, or seven years' providentiall absence, being not heard of . . . [and] counted as legally dead."[3]

Introduction

Connecticut Colony had the most liberal divorce policy in British America. Its courts heard approximately a thousand divorce cases during the course of the eighteenth century, far more than the courts of any other colony.[4] *Thrall* v. *Thrall* was one of the most hotly contested and therefore most richly documented cases; it was not, however, a typical case. Although most divorces involved de-

Alison Duncan Hirsch is in the doctoral program in American History at Columbia University.

43

sertion rather than (or in addition to) adultery, the husband was usually the deserter. Most deserting spouses left town, usually with a new lover and often for another colony altogether. Divorce proceedings in these cases were almost always uncontested, for often the respondent was not even notified of the complaint. Hannah Thrall, though, remained in Windsor; she simply returned to her parents' house, about two miles from her married home.[5] From that vantage point, she contested William at every turn. Although she sometimes declared in anger that she never wanted to live with William again, she clearly did not want to be sued for divorce, since she would lose all her dower rights if declared the guilty party.[6] William's estate was considerable, and her thirds would make her a fairly wealthy widow.

Hannah might have sued William for divorce herself on the grounds of cruelty, but only life-threatening abuse was sufficient cause for a special appeal to the General Assembly acting as a court of equity.[7] Hannah was thus consigned to a waiting role. In the early stages of her absence, William occasionally invited her to return home, but she refused to believe his promises to treat her better. For whatever combination of motives—wounded pride, malice, or a desire to be freed from an unpleasant relationship—William soon began to contemplate divorce. Since divorce on the grounds of desertion required a three-year wait, William accused Hannah of adultery, but he produced no convincing evidence. The other possible grounds for divorce, fraudulent contract, was out of the question from the beginning. This term covered impotence, previous marriage (bigamy), and previous fornication with another (usually revealed through obvious pregnancy too soon after marriage). Hannah and William had already proved their fertility by bearing a child, and any previous relationship of hers would have been known to him, since they had grown up together. If he wanted a divorce, then, William had no choice but to wait the full three years.

During the waiting period (which extended to five years because of various delays), this couple's marital discord gradually drew the entire Thrall clan and much of the community into the fray, opening old wounds of factionalism and rivalry and creating new ones. The scandal—for such it was to become—would seriously affect the fortunes of the Thrall family, which had been on the brink of joining the colony's elite. It would also have repercussions among several other Windsor families, as other couples in the town followed the

Thrall example and took their marital difficulties to court. What seemed at first to be an entirely private matter, an internal family squabble, became a highly public issue, with multiple reverberations in the society at large.

An essay of this scope can only hint at the relationship between specific families and communities, but the Thrall family crisis suggests that this relationship is an important key to understanding women's roles in communal life, a role ignored in most colonial town studies. Many women's historians, on the other hand, have tended to focus on actions women took as individuals: writing diaries, conducting their own businesses, or leaving wills.[8] Most women, like Hannah Thrall, were forced to participate in the larger world through the medium of the family, and rarely with more impact than in the course of a family's disintegration.

Historians have used colonial court records to explore two aspects of women's lives, their legal standing and their social and familial experience. Nancy Cott, for example, has analyzed both aspects, using the records of all divorces in eighteenth-century Massachusetts.[9] Divorce records are highly suggestive for women's historians. Men were far more frequent participants in the commercial, political, and criminal activities that usually landed people in court. Divorce records in this sense are unique: by definition they involve equal numbers of men and women.[10] By using these and other court records, as opposed to statutes, historians can demonstrate the actual workings of the law: what people knew about it, how they used it, how the courts applied it.[11]

Rather than take a statistical approach to divorce records as Cott and others have done, I have chosen to do a case study of one divorce trial, in the belief that such a concentrated focus can best reveal the actual experiences of colonial Connecticut families. I have reconstructed the sequence of events in this drama through the trial's petitions and depositions, supplemented by the traditional sources of the genealogist: vital records, wills, and other public records.[12]

The obvious difficulty in reconstructing events through court testimony is that participants present self-serving, often contradictory evidence. Under the rigid strictures of Puritan morality, witnesses rarely told outright lies; more often, they told partial truths, either because they did not remember the whole truth or pretended not to, or because they had scrupulously avoided discovering it. Witnesses cited conversations out of context and generally remembered only what they wanted to remember, so that —*Rashomon* fashion—several witnesses described the same event in utterly different fashions. Only by balancing the various accounts can we guess what really happened. Whenever Hannah's or William's version seems equally plausible, I have tended to accept the majority opinion of the community and the colonial authorities.

In the process of giving testimony, witnesses also gave evidence of a different sort, evidence for historians rather than judges. Enmeshed in partisan accounts of adultery and cruelty are casual references to things taken for granted in a colonial town: a group of young men breaks into a house at night to look for "the girls," and no one seems to mind; a grandmother offers to tend a sick child while the mother attends church, and neither thinks to ask the father. Participants thus unwittingly bare intimate details of their lives that would rarely be mentioned in letters or diaries. As Alan Macfarlane has noted, "In a sense it is the things that are unmentioned by the [literary] sources, the unmentionable, or assumptions that are too basic or obvious to need stating, which are of paramount interest to the historian."[13]

This essay, then, is an attempt to bring one small corner of the eighteenth century to life. The story of one family, and of one crisis within that family, can contribute little toward generalizations about colonial life. but it may, in a way, teach us more. The individual characters in this drama are both typical and atypical, both ordinary and extraordinary, as individuals always are. The Thralls represent their society primarily as deviants, as people who could not stay within the bounds of eighteenth-century respectability. Yet the very "biographical density" of their tale offers us a clearer vision of the place, the time, and the people.[14]

The Thrall Family of Windsor

By the 1730s, the town of Windsor was a hundred years old and had a population of two or three thousand. Located where the Farmington River runs into the Connecticut, the town's location and fertile soil made it ideal for the production and export of surplus agricultural goods. The region also provided valuable natural resources: minerals, lumber, and fish from the rivers.[15]

This favorable geography attracted the early Windsor settlers, who came in three separate groups arriving simultaneously in 1635 from Plymouth Colony, England, and Dorchester, Massachusetts. From the start, the Dorchester group provided most of the town's leadership. Dorchester men and their descendents provided the town's military, religious, and political leaders and became the town's wealthiest citizens.[16]

The Thrall family was not of this group. William Thrall and his wife (whose first name is unknown), the great-grandparents of William and Hannah, settled in Windsor the year after the town's founding. Their origins are unclear. Because they arrived after the first land distribution, they received slightly inferior land. Like most Windsor men, William undoubtedly was primarily a farmer, exporting surplus products like meat and grain to the West Indies and elsewhere. He also was something of an entrepreneur, operating a rock quarry in town. William Thrall was one of the few men outside the original Dorchester group to be chosen as a selectman, but unlike most selectmen did not go on to become a deputy to the General Assembly. He reached the fringe of the town's elite, but never achieved full membership in it.[17]

William and Hannah's common grandfather, Timothy Thrall, was also more than a mere farmer, for he ran a fishing enterprise in the Connecticut River. He was also a bit of a troublemaker in the religious upheavals of the time. In the 1670s, he gained some notoriety—as a leader of the dissenting Second Church in Windsor. In 1680 he and his fellow dissenters were fined for "defamation of authority" because of a "scandalous and offensive" letter they had sent the governor.[18]

The Thrall family achieved its greatest prominence in its third generation in America. William's father, Timothy Thrall, Jr., became a captain in the militia, the highest local military office, and served as a deputy to the General Assembly for four years. Like his forbears he was an entrepreneur: he was a partner in an ironworks and owned a large general store.[19] He married into one of Windsor's most prominent families, the Allyns. His inheritance, his marriage, and his various enterprises made Captain Timothy Thrall a wealthy man. When Timothy died in 1724, he left his "Loving Wife " Sarah the sum of £500 "to be to her forever." More important for later events, she was also to have "the use of half my house, orchards, and homested during her widowhood."[20]

Sarah Thrall received a larger portion of the house than did most

Windsor widows: the usual practice was one-third.[21] When Timothy died, William was still single and had little use for a larger part of the homestead; when he had a wife and child living there the situation may have become awkward. In addition, Sarah's widowhood continued longer than most: she survived her husband by seventeen years, dying at the age of seventy-four, and she never remarried.[22]

Although William did not receive the usual double portion allotted eldest sons, his inheritance was substantial. He inherited his father's ironworks share and probably the general store as well. The numerous plots of Thrall land, scattered throughout Windsor and the surrounding towns, were divided equally between William and his brother, Timothy, Jr., then twelve years old. Their two sisters, like their mother, received £500 in personal property.[23]

Hannah's father, Thomas Thrall, left much less in the way of records than did his brother, Timothy. His wife, Elizabeth Haskins, was from a much less prominent family. Thomas and Elizabeth neglected to record the birth of their firstborn child, and when Thomas died intestate no probate records were even made, perhaps because there was no surviving son. Hannah's only brother died early; she was the second of four daughters.[24]

Marriage and Desertion

According to the town vital records, William and Hannah Thrall were married on October 11, 1728, but their daughter, Charity, seems to have been born about 1725. Apparently the Thralls either had a common-law marriage or indulged in that favorite Puritan sin and crime, fornication.[25] In 1727 the town constable came to Thomas Thrall's house to serve Hannah with a writ for some unspecified offense; the crime may well have been fornication, the most common transgression for a young woman. Thomas Thrall's reaction is also suggestive: the angry father kicked the constable out of the house.[26] The family had other wayward members at the same time: a mutual cousin, John Thrall, was said to have fathered an illegitimate child in 1724.[27]

The records do not indicate whether the family forced the couple to marry or whether they did so by choice. Marriages between first cousins were of dubious morality, but they were on the rise in eighteenth-century New England. Authorities debated the issue, but Connecticut never seems to have expressly forbidden such unions as other colonies did.[28] The records remain silent on how Hannah and William's marriage was received and on whether or not the couple was happy at first. All we can tell is that in the three and a half years of their legitimate married life together, they had no further children—a fact worth noting because of the remarkable regularity with which most New England couples bore children at two-year intervals.[29]

Whatever their early relationship, it seems to have soured in the months before Hannah left, although friends and relatives gave conflicting reports. One neighbor testified that William had been a good husband before all the trouble began: in April 1732 Hannah told Eunice Stoughton how kind William was being to her while she was sick.[30] Other testimony suggests that Eunice quoted Hannah out of context: perhaps Hannah actually noted how unusual a single kindness from William was. At the end of May, after she had left home, Hannah told a group of people that Eunice and her husband knew quite well that William had behaved badly. Cousin John Thrall testified:

> She told us her husband used her so Cruely as that she bein so sick as to be Confined to her Chamber about a fortnight and her husband allowed her no help onely his negro boy and Charity to bring a litell water and injon [Indian] meal to mack porig and had nothing els to liv on and She furder said John Stoughton and his wife and sundry others Co[u]ld Say the Same but they have not speek.[31]

William's neglect was all the more pointed because there were many other people in the household who could have helped besides the children: four adult black slaves, one Indian servant, one apprentice, William's mother, his brother (then about nineteen), and, of course, William himself.[32]

If William did not take care of Hannah while she was sick, he still expected her to care for his needs once she was better. On Monday evening, two days before she left him, he asked her for his meal. Perhaps remembering how little she had been given to eat during her illness, she replied that she had nothing for him. This was not the first time Hannah had refused to perform her housewifely chores: William claimed that "it had been usual for her to neglect in a great degree the womans Duty of this kind," and asked, "Who can live with such a woman?" The following night, election day, the couple quarreled again. William struck Hannah and told her to "be gone out of his house." The next day she did just that.[33]

These were the incidents that Hannah claimed had driven her from home. William and his supporters told a different story. Sarah Thrall testified that there had been no quarrel at all between her son and daughter-in-law, and the two men who witnessed Hannah's departure said that her only reason for leaving was that she wanted to live apart from her mother-in-law. John Stoughton (Eunice's husband) and George Bradley of Tolland were visiting William on the day after elections in May 1732, they said, when Hannah came into the room with a bundle of clothes under her arm and "declared She was a Going away from her Husband, and She would not live with him Except said William would gett his Mother out of the House or goe and Live in another House." Furthermore, she had a place "to Board att" and intended to "Work at her Trade" (probably sewing), to which her husband replied that "if She could Work abroad he Thought She might at Home and he wanted or would have her finish the WasteCoat she began some Years ago." Stoughton and Bradley both claimed to have "Endeavored to perswaid her to Stay" in the interest of preserving peace in the Thrall family and thereby in the community.[34]

The community and even the colony soon heard of the family's troubles, however. William's notoriety must have had something to do with the General Assembly's refusal in May 1732 to commission him as a captain in the militia, even though he had been elected by the men in his company to follow in his father's footsteps and was in line for the promotion. The Assembly rarely made such refusals, but a man who could not even control his own wife was hardly capable of commanding a militia company. The records give no reason for the ruling against William, but the Assembly was adamant that Samuel Mather, who wished to resign, should "lead his company" in making a more appropriate choice than Thrall.[35] Mather himself may have had some quarrel with William and spoken against him; he was to play an important role in the divorce proceedings—on Hannah's side.

Earlier Divorce Trials

When Hannah made it clear that she would not readily return home, William must have begun to consider his alternatives. As a merchant-farmer, an educated man, and a frequent participant in litigation, William was no doubt aware of the divorce laws.[36] He may well have known about divorce on a more personal level, through acquaintance with other Windsor families who had divorced members.

Divorce, of course, was far from unknown in Connecticut. Besides the comparatively broad grounds for divorce, Connecticut divorces were nearly always absolute (*a vinculo*), in other words, with permission to remarry. Other colonies more often granted mere legal separations, or divorce from bed and board (*a mensa et thoro*).[37] The biblical commonwealth of Connecticut, like Massachusetts, inherited its divorce theory from a long line of Calvinist and Puritan theorists going back two centuries. Civil authorities turned to local clergy for advice on divorce policy and, once that policy was set, continued to request the opinion of ministerial committees in unusually troublesome cases.

To Puritans, divorce—although by no means to be encouraged—was a necessary mechanism for keeping family relationships orderly, and order was of the highest importance in New England towns. A controlled divorce policy, it was thought, would prevent the clandestine and bigamous marriages said to be rampant in England due to the difficulty of obtaining legal divorces.[38] By permitting remarriage, divorce would keep men and women from succumbing to the temptations that beset deserted spouses. The morals of deserting spouses were of far less concern: usually deserters could not even be located. William, of course, was not so lucky: Hannah's continued presence in Windsor meant that both sides of the case would be aired.

The Thralls' divorce controversy was not the first to disrupt Windsor society: between 1694 and 1725, the courts heard at least five divorce suits involving one or both spouses from Windsor.[39] The most infamous marital dispute involved the respected Stoughton family and served as a pretext for struggles over ministerial prerogatives in East Windsor parish. In 1724 Abigail Stoughton married John Moore, Jr., reportedly a profligate young man, without her father's permission. Her father, Thomas Stoughton, who was the brother-in-law of East Windsor minister Timothy Edwards, asked the church to mediate and decide whether the marriage was valid. Individual congregations frequently attempted to resolve all sorts of disputes, particularly for prominent families.[40]

Without first consulting the lay leaders of the congregation, the usual procedure, Edwards brought the matter before the Hartford North Association of clergy, which decided that in such cases the father had the right to invalidate the marriage. Abigail went home to her father's house, and her would-be husband took the case to court, asking either for the marriage to be declared valid or for a legitimate annulment. The court held that the marriage was binding, finding no basis in the statutes for the decision of the clerical association. (Timothy Edwards, who was, incidentally, the father of Jonathan, was also to play a role in the Thralls' problems. He had personal experience with divorce: at the age of nineteen he had testified on his father's behalf in a successful divorce suit accusing his mother of adultery.)[41]

Of greatest significance to the Thrall case, because it also involved a wife's desertion, was a 1717 incident involving yet another prominent Windsor family, the Newberrys. Hannah Newberry, the well-off widow of Windsor's Benjamin Newberry,[42] married widower John Merriman of Wallingford but left him soon afterward. According to Hannah, before their marriage John agreed that she would maintain control of her own estate, but immediately after the wedding he pressed her to hand over her property and threatened her so that she feared for her life. He had also promised that she would not have much work to do in her new home, but it proved to require "exceeding hard service" since there was little household help.[43] To counter her arguments, John produced in court a deposition by six servants in his household as well as copies of letters he had sent to Hannah after her return to Windsor, in which he requested her to come back and even promised to make her job easier by sending away some or all of his children.[44]

In March 1717 Merriman brought his suit for divorce before the General Assembly, which referred the case to the Superior Court meeting in New Haven the following year. The court requested the opinion of a committee of clergymen, apparently because the problem of a wife deserting, without simultaneously committing adultery, had never before come up. Desertion had until then been construed to mean desertion by the husband; that a wife would or could desert was a new concept.[45] Women were considered powerless to control their husbands and therefore required the protection of the law. Men, on the other hand, were supposed to be able to maintain control over their wives, presumably both physically and financially. However, because Puritanism did not condone physical abuse of wives, and because some widows had considerable means of their own, the husband's control often had to be based solely on mutual affection.[46]

John Merriman demonstrated to everyone's satisfaction that he had behaved as a Puritan husband should. The ministers pronounced that a civil divorce was allowable in the Merriman case because, by her desertion, Hannah had in effect employed the Hebraic method of self-divorce. Therefore it was only "Orderly" for the authorities to release John Merriman from his matrimonial bonds.[47] The court followed their advice and granted the divorce, citing "the indefatigable care and pains that has been taken by the said Merriman to seduce her."[48] Twenty years later, the court would search for the same "care and pains" in William Thrall's behavior—and fail to find them.

The Church Hearing

Before going to court William could approach another forum, the church. The church, of course, could not grant a divorce or even a legal separation as English ecclesiastical courts could, but it could mediate disputes, assess guilt, and impose various sanctions. It could require the guilty party to confess to the injured party and the congregation for disrupting the community. If a church member failed to submit to its discipline, the congregation could vote to censure or, as a last resort, to excommunicate.[49]

In August 1732, William went before the Windsor First Society and "exhibited a charge against [Hannah] of the scandalous violation of the Seventh, Eighth and Ninth Commands," thus accusing her simultaneously of adultery, desertion, and slander. Aside from sheer irrational anger, William had two possible motives: he hoped either that the church would order his wife to return or that its members would convict her of adultery so that he could sue for divorce without delay. Whatever his goal, things did not go the way he planned. He had scant evidence of adultery: he does not seem to have named any specific partner. He probably counted on the Puritan suspicion of a woman (or a man) who lived apart from his or her spouse. The church members discussed the matter for some time and then requested the opinion of a committee of ministers from neighboring towns, all members of the Hartford North Association.[50]

The committee did not act immediately. In the meantime, William was unable to control his temper. Hannah's mother, Elizabeth Thrall, testified that in September 1732 he came 'to our house . . . seemingly in a grate passion Saying you Divilish Bitch I have heard Enough what you have said about me and with that Laid hold of the hair of her head and pulled her to the Dore and Struck her and Kicked her Severall times." That evening Hannah went to visit Captain Samuel Mather, a Windsor justice of the peace, "to take advice," presumably as to her legal options.[51] No record remains of Mather's advice, but judging from Hannah's subsequent behavior he probably told her to do nothing and let William hang himself.

After her initial assertive act of deserting (assertive only in the most limited sense), Hannah's role was essentially reactive, the appropriate stance for a Puritan woman. As a woman, and an illiterate one at that, Hannah probably had far less knowledge of the law than William and needed male advice.[52] She allowed men—justices of the peace, ministers, male relatives and neighbors—to take her defense. Witnesses to meetings between William and Hannah quoted his words, rarely hers, suggesting that she let him do the talking. His words and actions were indeed the critical factor in his defeat.

While Hannah was at Captain Mather's seeking advice, William confronted her again. He brought in Israel Ashley and cousin John Thrall as witnesses that he "requested" and "commanded" her to go home to "his" house.[53] Hannah did in fact return a few days later to take care of her sick daughter, then about seven years old, who had remained with William, since he had custody according to Connecticut law.[54] Hannah's mother testified:

> I went down to See the Child Charity, She being not well, and as I Sat holding the Child in my lap, his wife being there at the same time . . . after in the evening William Thrall Came home and I asked William Thrall why he kept the Chamber dore Bolted or Locked that we Could not get in for we wanted to Carry the Child to Bed and he made me no Reply and then I asked him again and told him that it would be better I thought for his Wife to go to bed and take the Child to bed with her. His answer was to me that his wife should not Tarry there. She may go away—the Child hearing her fathers Rash Answer fell a Sitting and Sobing and for all her husband said to her, his wife, she should not tarry there yet she did Notwithstanding

untill the Child was got to Sleep and then being Shut out of her Bed Room She went away to Lodge.[55]

Elizabeth's testimony implies no censure of William for not taking care of Charity himself; obviously that was a "womans Duty."[56] She does, however, reproach him for keeping mother and daughter from each other and for arguing in front of the child. We should note that, on this occasion at least, Charity's paternal grandmother was uninvolved with her granddaughter's care, either from lack of concern or out of spitefulness against the child's mother. In fact, Sarah Thrall could be counted on so little that the other grandmother apparently stayed overnight after Hannah left, for the next day Elizabeth had no Sunday clothes to wear:

> It being Sabath Day I Said to William Thralls wife I haveing not Cloth[e]s there I would Tend the Child in the forenoon and She might go to Meeting and upon that William Thralls wife asked her husband for her Cloth[e]s in order to go to Meeting and her husband would not Let her have them and She was forced to borrow Clothes to go to Meeting.[57]

William's behavior was directly contrary to the Puritan concept of marriage, in which the husband had certain duties toward his wife as well as rights over her.[58] When the case came to court, therefore, he attempted to show that the incident had been quite different: he had actually encouraged Hannah to stay. Sarah Thrall testified that William had asked her to prepare a bed for Hannah, but there was a question of which bed. Thomas Moses, who had been living in the house at the time, no doubt as a servant or apprentice, quoted William as saying "sundry times" that "She Should not Lye in the house where he Lived . . . unless She Lay in the bed where Robon Indian Lay and Shitt in."[59] A former servant of Thomas Thrall's also testified against his own household. Othniel Gillet stated that during this time William often came to ask Hannah to come home, telling her that "She Should never want for nothing so Long as he Lived."[60]

At this early stage in their separation, both William and Hannah seemed to act with some ambivalence, but later, when the case actually went to trial, it was important for each of them to show that he or she had always been willing to be reconciled. It was important for William to prove that he had done his utmost to gain his wife back, for that was a husband's duty. It was crucial for Hannah to prove that she had deserted for good cause: her financial future was at stake.

The ministerial committee, which included Timothy Edwards of East Windsor, finally met for a hearing in June 1733 and again in early 1734. On both occasions Hannah insisted that when she left William she had only intended to stay away until he calmed down. William's temper got the better of him even before the ministers, who perceived that the "Tenour of his behaviour, . . . his Sharp biting and reproachful reflections on her, particularly before this Church now" made all her accusations about his previous behavior believable. The ministers concluded that adultery charges could not be proven against Hannah, that William was guilty of "Shewing his exceeding great Aversion to her, and rendering her hopes of the comfort of A Wife in him desperate," and that "the blame of the Seperation" lay mainly with him. Quoting the English Puritan theologian William Ames, they wrote, "Dr. Ames in his *Cases of Conscience* asserts that if a man by hard usage and cruel treatment drive his wife away from him or neglect her necessary departure and use not proper means to recover her, he is to be esteemed the Desertor."[61]

The day after their second meeting, the ministers went to William's house to reason with him once more, but "he Express'd himself fully Resolved never to take his wife any more." The ministers issued their opinion on February 13, 1734, and it was ratified by "most of the Brethren then present." Two weeks later, a meeting of all voting members of the congregation approved the statement.[62]

Divorce Proceedings

William now had no choice but to wait the full three years after Hannah's departure before he could sue for divorce. In the meantime, the Thralls' marital problems came before the courts in a different way. Soon after the congregation acquitted her in early 1734, Hannah asked her father's permission to bring Charity to live in his house. When he agreed, she in effect kidnapped her daughter from William. William immediately brought suit before the county court, not for child custody but for monetary damages.[63] He could not sue Hannah, since she was still legally his wife and "covered" by his legal identity, so he sued her father. The jury awarded William total damages of one shilling, probably judging that he was legally right but morally wrong. Charity was then eight or nine years old, an age by which daughters had already begun to receive fairly intensive training in domestic chores from their mothers.[64] The only woman at William's house who could have provided such training was Sarah Thrall, who, as we have seen, was not much help with her granddaughter. By all standards except the customary legal rights of a father over his child, Charity was better off with her mother.

William, however, was enraged by the jury's decision and used it as a pretext for embroiling Thomas in litigation for the next six months. Several small debts on either side aggravated the friction between nephew and uncle. Once again, members of the community stepped in to try to bring order, but their efforts compounded the problem. "Som friends who Desired the Peace of the familys Perswaded us to Put that mater and also all other Differences to arbitration," Thomas testified. When the arbitrators did not award William as much money as he thought he deserved, he managed to have Thomas arrested and put in jail. Citing "all the Trubell and Cost He Hath Put me to about this Trifling Bisnes," Thomas appealed to the General Assembly meeting in New Haven in October 1734. The Assembly ordered William to desist.[65]

In August 1735, after the requisite three years had passed, an incident occurred that enabled William to charge Hannah in court with adultery as well as desertion. Samuel Palmer gave a lurid description of the goings on one night at Thomas Thrall's house, when he and two other young men were visiting:

> Aron [Pinney] and Hannah Thrall withdrew from the company and went into the Chamber where there was a bed and after some time I called to have Aron Penny come down and he did not come and thereupon I went partly Up the stairs and saw Hannah Thrall Lying on the bed with her coats Up so high that I did see her Naked lages and Aron Penny Lying on her belly seeming to Lye on her belly some times more Uneasie than others as it seemed to me that he prest hard towards her body and secret parts with suden Motions.[66]

His testimony was confirmed, in more circumspect terms, by Moses Griswold:

Going partly up the Chamber Stairs nigh the top of said Stairs I heard a whispering and I judged they was on the bed in said Chamber . . . and I went away . . . it being in the night Season and Dark [so] that I could not Se anything what their actions was.[67]

Elizabeth Thrall, Jr., Hannah's sister, gave quite a different version of the story. It all began, apparently, because Hannah was not a very proper hostess. She had been folding clean laundry in the main room of the house while they had company, and Elizabeth reminded her that this was not proper and that their mother would be too embarrassed to come into the room. Hannah announced that she would carry the laundry up to the chamber, or bedroom.

Then said Palmer spoke unto the aforesaid Pinney and told him that he would give him a Tankor of Punch to go up into the Chamber and Court Capt. Thralls Wife and accordingly said Pinney went up Chamber and presently after I Heard Sister Hannah Call to Samuel Palmer and bid him Run now if he Intended to Do Capt. Thrall any Good, for Aaron Pinney had farely flong her on the beds, and Palmer Run upstares and they all Came Downstares together.[68]

Aaron Pinney, who may have been Hannah's cousin, confirmed Elizabeth's evidence, since he obviously did not want to be accused of adultery. Palmer's evidence was pretty well undercut by his answer to one simple question asked by Windsor Justice of the Peace Samuel Mather: "Q: did you offer to give Aaron Pinny a Tanker of punch if he would goe up Chamber with Capt. Thralls wife? A: yes." Abigail Stevens, Jr., said that Palmer told her that after the incident he went to look for Captain Thrall to tell him the "good news" about having seen Hannah in bed with some one. Not finding him at home, he went to Hoyte's Meadow, where, Palmer told Abigail, "Thrall bid me Get up Behind him . . . and he brought me Down to his . . . House and he gave me as much Lickor as I could Drink which was all that I told the story to him for."[69]

On August 25, 1735, William filed his petition with the Superior Court scheduled to meet in Hartford on the second Tuesday in September. Justice of the Peace Henry Allyn immediately sent an order to Constable Benjamin Griswold (the father of Moses), who notified the court that he had read the petition and summons to Hannah. She thus had only a few days to prepare her case. Soon after she received the summons, Hannah or one of her allies asked Timothy Edwards for assistance, and on September 9 he penned the only deposition for either side filed at this time. Edwards recounted the process by which the ministers' committee had come to its decision censuring William, laying special stress on Hannah's expression of willingness to return to William and William's refusal to take her back.[70]

William's petition carefully followed the formula found in most Connecticut petitions. He gave the date of his marriage to Hannah and the date of her desertion and prayed that their marriage be declared "Nul and void and that your memorialist be Discharged from all marrage Dutys towards said Hannah etc., according to the Laws of the Colony in Such Cases made and Provided."[71] The petition mentions only the charge of desertion, but later court records and depositions indicate that he also charged her with adultery.

William seems to have told Samuel Palmer's story to the court himself, expecting the judges to rely solely on hearsay; it is possible that the court requested further testimony when it postponed any action until the next session in Hartford in March 1736. William at least had not traveled to Hartford for nothing: another civil case was decided in his favor, although still another was postponed along with the divorce suit.[72]

No mention of the divorce case appears in the court records for March 1736, perhaps because William was sick at the time and unable to attend. There may have even been a temporary reconciliation when Hannah returned to his house during his illness, though William's brother, Timothy, testified that Hannah "Went a Way presently and Never did Nothing for him as I no on."[73] Hannah's visit might have been inspired by financial considerations rather than (or combined with) concern for William. Windsor men customarily made wills only in old age, unless they were sick or departing on a military expedition,[74] and William, though only thirty-six, was so sick he feared he was dying. Hannah may have visited him to make sure that she would be included in his will. Instead he virtually cut her out when he wrote his will on June 9, 1736.[75]

In most Windsor wills, a husband mentioned his wife first if she was still living, but William's first bequest was to his "Honoured Mother Sarah," who was to inherit a "Negro Girl Called Pegg" and

£25 in money. It was not a large bequest, but not because of a lack of affection: Sarah was already in possession of a comfortable living from her widow's thirds.[76] The second bequest, to Hannah, was an insult: "the sum of Ten Shillings Money." No adjective such as "loving" or "respected" modified her name as it usually did for wives in the formalized language of eighteenth-century wills.[77] William could not possibly have been ignorant of the common law and Connecticut statutory provision that a widow could claim her thirds instead of the bequest specified in her husband's will.[78] The law was designed to prevent just this sort of spiteful neglect of a widow, lest the widow be stranded without means and therefore dependent on the good will—and slim funds—of her community. William must have known that Hannah would have the courts overturn his will; he just wanted to threaten her or to make things difficult for her even after his death.

William was far more generous toward his daughter, Charity. She was to receive £500 at age eighteen or upon marriage. As a further slight to Hannah, William stipulated that his brother, Timothy, should be Charity's guardian—a rather impractical decision, since Timothy was then only twenty-three and still unmarried. Besides other bequests of £25 each to one sister (the other had already died) and to seven nieces and nephews, William left everything else to Timothy, who was also designated executor. This marked a final slight to Hannah, since many Windsor men of the period named their wives as executors, or at least as co-executors with a male relative.[79]

There is no way of knowing whether Hannah was aware of this will before William's death two and a half years later, although he may have taunted her with it. The only ones who definitely knew of it were three witnesses: his neighbor John Stoughton (also a witness in the divorce trial); fellow townsman Ezekiel Bissell; and town clerk John McMoran.[80]

William's illness did not prevent his friends from looking for more indications of adultery on Hannah's part. Now thirty-four, she was again reported to be flirting with younger men. Between March and May 1736, Noadiah Gillet and Hannah created suspicions by being too intimate with each other. Abraham Pinney, a first cousin to both William and Hannah, and Abel Griswold testified that in March 1736 "[Charles] Phelps said to [Noadiah] Gillet that he [i.e. Gillet] went up into Chamber to have to do with Hannah Thrall and abel Griswold asked said Gillet if She would fuck wel and [he] said Aye or yes Like a mink."[81] The statement—obviously obscured by bad grammar—seems to be merely an example of young men bragging about sexual exploits that may or may not have been real.

Noadiah Phelps testified that on two occasions in April he saw Hannah and Noadiah Gillet "in a Close and famillior Conversation," once while they sat on a fence near a well by Thomas Thrall's house and once "In a Remote Corner of the House behind the Grate Table."[82] He called attention to the fact that these incidents had taken place in the evening and that both times he did not see Gillet for the rest of the night, but the testimony actually contained no proof of adulterous behavior.

The most damaging incident occurred in May, according to another young man, John Owen, Jr. He was walking home one night with Noadiah Gillet and David Thrall when they passed by Thomas Thrall's house. According to Owen:

> Gillet made a motion to go in. I told him 'twas Late and better to keep a Long but however we went in and a Motion being made where the Girls was and where hannah phelps was, there or no, whereupon said Gillet Lighted up a Candle and said he would, *he would* find them and said David Thrall said he thought hannah Thrall was abed in the Chamber and Said Gillet went up into said Chamber and talked to Some Body, I judged to said hannah Thrall, and asked her where hannah phelps was, there or no. Shee Said no, etc., and I occationally Staying till near morning I went and Rap[p]ed upon the under Side of the Chamber flowr but hearing no noise I went away and Left him with said Hannah Thrall, as I Judged, in said Chamber, and Said Gillet told me afterwards he Slept there the bigest part of the said night.[83]

Until the end of the eighteenth century it was not at all unusual for people, even unrelated people of opposite sexes, to sleep in the same room without engaging in any sort of sexual relationship.[84] Noadiah Gillet gave an explanation along these lines to Benjamin Griswold, Jr., who met him one day on the road. In the typical, socially responsible—or nosy—fashion of an eighteenth-century New Englander, Griswold asked him what all the rumors were about.

He gave me sum acount. I answered him it may be if he [Owen] had gon into the chamber he might have seen you in bed with her. He answered me he thought that he wont have seen him on the bed by her for [he] said he iwent into the chamber five feet and lay down on the bed by her and in a little time fell asleep and did not wake till near break of day.[85]

From their behavior, it seems that the young men had all been drinking, and Gillet seems to have claimed that he simply passed out in Hannah's room. It was a rather weak explanation, but the court apparently accepted it. John Owen's credibility may have been questionable because he failed to mention why he himself stayed in the house until morning, nor did David Thrall give any account of his whereabouts. Perhaps one of them spent the night with Hannah Phelps, the sister of Noadiah Phelps, probably a servant in Thomas Thrall's household.

The men involved in this escapade, as well as those participating in the earlier "adultery" incident involving Aaron Pinney, were all in their late teens or early twenties and may well have been members of the militia company that had selected William as captain. Despite the refusal of colonial officials to commission him, they continued to call him "captain" among themselves.[86] Their support of him in his personal troubles may reflect a sort of hero-worship. Perhaps his violent temper and even his penchant for wife-abuse appealed to this rowdy bunch of young men who liked to drink heavily and go looking for "girls."

These two incidents reveal the precarious situation of unmarried women, even those living within their fathers' households, in an era of unlocked doors and young men relatively unfettered by traditional moral codes. The rise in premarital sex during the eighteenth century may have been caused more by the lifting of restraints from the behavior of young men than, as some historians have suggested,[87] by the rebellion of young women against their parents.

The rumors about Noadiah and Hannah may have been true; after four years of separation from her husband, she might have had enough of celibacy. If Noadiah was carrying on with Hannah, she was not the only one. In the following year, he married Sarah Owen, and their son Noadiah, Jr., was born only two months after the wedding.[88]

Two depositions on William's behalf were filed with the court in

time for its September 1736 session: George Bradley and Israel
Ashley testified before justices of the peace in Tolland, Connecticut, and Westfield, Massachusetts, respectively.[89] Once again the
case was not heard, although another Windsor divorce petition was
granted in that session. Abigail Stevens petitioned the court for a
divorce from her husband, John, who seven years earlier had "Left
the Town of Windsor and I suppose New England."[90] There was no
further testimony in this case, and the court granted the divorce
without delay. The more troublesome Thrall case, however, was
postponed, probably with a request for further evidence, for immediately after the court adjourned a series of depositions was filed in
Windsor.

Seven witnesses filed depositions on behalf of William on four
separate occasions between September 23 and October 2, 1736. The
first six—his mother, Sarah; his brother, Timothy; his cousin John;
Zabud and Giddeon Gillet, who were brothers; and their cousin,
Othniel Gillet—testified before Justice of the Peace Henry Allyn,
who was William's first cousin on his mother's side but unrelated by
blood to Hannah. Allyn notified Hannah of each witness's scheduled appearance, but he did not record any rebuttals she might have
made. He wrote only, "Hannah Thrall of Windsor being notified
and present" (or "but not present" on one occasion).[91] Hannah's
responses, however, were recorded when one of William's witnesses, Samuel Palmer, testified before the other Windsor justice of
the peace, Samuel Mather, who had earlier befriended her. Mather
noted Hannah's presence and added that she "denied all that is
written in this evidence Except that Aaron Pinney was with her in
the Chamber and followed her up into the Chamber, She being
going up to Carey Some linnen."[92] Although these justices did not
display any blatant prejudice, it seems clear that Allyn favored William's side and Mather, Hannah's. With the sole exception of
Palmer, witnesses appeared before the justice more sympathetic to
their side.

The four witnesses who filed depositions for Hannah between
October 4 and October 17 all went before Samuel Mather. William
was notified but did not appear on any of the three occasions.
Aaron Pinney and Elizabeth Thrall, Jr., filed a joint deposition
telling their version of the first "adultery" incident. The other
witnesses were John Moses, William's former servant and possibly
a mutual cousin from Simsbury, and Abigail Stevens, Jr., the nine-

teen-year-old daughter of the woman who had just obtained a
divorce. Abigail related a conversation she had had with Hannah
the previous month. Hannah came to visit and Abigail asked her
how things had gone at court. When Hannah told her that William
had brought up Samuel Palmer's story, Abigail suggested that they
go to Thomas Allyn's house (where Palmer either worked or lived)
to ask Palmer "what he had to say for himself." It was on this
occasion that Palmer declared he had only told the story to get
some "Lickor." Palmer's version of the incident, included in his
deposition of October 2, was that Hannah had asked him to come
see her at Abigail's house and begged him not to say anything
about the Pinney episode, for, he said, "If I told of it her husband
might get quit from her which might prove to her ruine for that
she should have no Intrest [in her] Husbands Estates."[93]

Eight additional witnesses filed written statements on behalf of
William when the court actually convened to hear the case on May
25, 1737: Eunice and John Stoughton, John Owen, Jr., Moses Griswold, Abel Griswold, Noadiah Phelps, Daniel Pinney, and Abraham Pinney. After the vast array of testimony on both sides, the
decision of the magistrates was brief:

> This Court having heard and duely Considered the Pleas and
> Evidence by the said William Exhibited and Produced in Proof
> of the Matters of fact in his said Petition alledged, allso the
> Evidence by said Hannah produced in her Defence are of
> Opinion that they are not Sufficiently proved and do accord-
> ingly not Se cause to grant his said Petition or Separate or
> Divorce him from his said Wife as prayd for.[94]

William must have tried once more to obtain a divorce, for there
is a second petition dated March 1, 1738, and addressed to the
Superior Court meeting in Hartford that month.[95] There is no mention of this suit actually being heard.

William's suit may have been withdrawn when he discovered that
there were grounds on which Hannah could sue him for divorce. If
Esther Griswold's claims were to be believed, sometime in Decem-
ber 1737 or January 1738 she had become pregnant by William.
Then twenty-five years old, twelve years younger than William,
Esther was the sister of two deponents in the Thrall divorce trial.
She was still living at her father's house, where she gave birth to a

son on September 5, 1738. During her pregnancy and childbirth she had identified William as the father. According to law and custom, a woman was supposed to be able to speak only the truth about the identity of the father during her labor, and a man so identified was usually convicted of fornication and/or successfully sued for child support, or maintenance as it was called. Esther named the boy William, no doubt as a further indication of his parentage. Esther testified that soon after her delivery William had visited her at her father's house and "freley Confesed Himself to Be the father of said Childe and Declared that He Would Suport said Child."[96]

Esther's situation changed for the worse when William died on October 25, 1738, for he had made no formal provision for the child's support. For Hannah, on the other hand, William's death must have brought a sense of relief, for it meant freedom from a marriage in which there was little chance of reconciliation, as well as the possibility of financial independence at the relatively young age of thirty-six.

Aftermath

Even after William's death, the problems spawned by this troubled marriage continued to plague his family, the courts, and the community. In December 1738 the will was probated and an inventory was exhibited by Timothy Thrall, the executor. Charity, then thirteen years old, chose her mother as her guardian, although William's will had specified otherwise.[97] The court accepted her decision since by her age a child had the right to select her own guardian.[98]

During the next year and a half Hannah fought in probate court to obtain her full dower rights. She accused Timothy of omitting "considerable of the estate . . . both bonds, notes, and lands" from the inventory. The court took her side, ordered Timothy to perfect the inventory, and appointed a committee of three men to set out her dower. By late 1740, when the matter was finally settled, Hannah Thrall was a fairly wealthy widow. Along with some twelve parcels of land in Windsor, she was given "the South East Half of said House [formerly Capt. Timothy Thrall's], viz: the Parlour, the Chamber and Garret above It and the Cellar, with Liberty to Pass up and Down the Stairs as there Shall be occasion."[99] This must have been the house she had lived in with William, and Sarah and Timothy Thrall were presumably the occupants of the other half of the house. (Timothy married in August 1740 and may have brought his wife there as well; Sarah died in December 1740.) It is difficult to imagine Hannah going back there to live unless both her mother-in-law and brother-in-law were gone. She may simply have stayed with Charity in her father's house until her remarriage.

On November 17, 1743, five years after William's death, Hannah married Joseph Hickox, a widower with six children. Several of his children were already married, but the youngest was only ten, so Hannah took on the responsibilities of a larger family. Hickox was not a wealthy man and seems to have been a tenant in Windsor rather than a freeholder.[100] A year after her mother's wedding, when she was only nineteen, Charity Thrall married Jonathan Alford, a young man from an old Windsor family of modest means.[101] In 1747 Joseph Hickox died; for her thirds Hannah received parcels of land in Goshen and Barkhempsted as well as moveable property totalling £30 6s 6p, the most valuable items being a feather bed and a quilt. When Hickox died, his only minor child chose a brother-in-law rather than his stepmother as his guardian. Hannah thus had no further responsibility for Hickox's children.[102] She may have gone to live with Charity and her husband, who by then had one child and were to have three more.

In 1763 Hannah was married a third time, to another first cousin, James Cornish of Simsbury, a neighboring town.[103] Cornish was a widower with seven grown children and many grandchildren. His family was a leading one in the town: he himself was a captain in the militia (the title that had eluded William Thrall), and his father had served as a deputy from Simsbury to the General Assembly at the same time as William's father had represented Windsor.[104]

Three years after the death of her only child from epidemic dysentery in 1776, Hannah Thrall died on August 27, 1779. In her will, the only surviving document that bears her name (she signed it with a mark), she wrote that she was "Sick of Body but of Sound mind and memory, Thanks be given to God the Wise." She bequeathed "all my ware, my Close, and all the Rest of my moveable Estate" to her two granddaughters, Charity Brown and Hannah Holcomb, because she had already given her two grandsons "all I Intend to Give Them."[105]

The Thrall family fortunes were thus dissipated to other families—the Alfords, the Browns, and the Holcombs—and the family's aspirations for membership in Connecticut's elite were effectively brought to a halt. Although this might have been due to social stigma because of the Thralls' problems, it was probably caused more by the simple fact that the couple had only one child, and that child was a daughter.

The community as well as the family experienced disruption. During the years in which the Thrall case occupied the courts and for ten years thereafter, there was a divorce case nearly every year involving Windsor men and women. Including the Thrall case, a total of eleven suits was brought in the years from 1736 to 1748.[106] As we have seen, there were only five cases before this, spanning the years 1694 to 1725; for the rest of the eighteenth century, there were only two more divorce cases in Windsor, both in the 1750s.[107] During the mid-century "epidemic," the divorce rate in Windsor far outpaced the average colonial rate for the period. Although divorce was still infrequent. the fact that it occurred in clusters meant that it had a greater impact in certain communities and at certain times than the overall statistics would indicate.[108]

Perhaps the Thrall case caused a contagion of divorces, setting off a chain reaction of unhappy spouses taking their troubles to the courts. The Thrall family affairs must have been a major topic of conversation wherever Windsor people gathered, and through this case townspeople would have become familiar with the uses and limitations of the divorce law and the court process.[109]

Besides the contagion effect, the divorce trauma of mid-century Windsor may have reflected a generally troubled society. Windsor First Society came through the Great Awakening of 1741–1742 relatively unscathed, along with most of Connecticut's older parishes, but East Windsor had its own peculiar ecclesiastical problems beginning in 1741. Once again, a woman from the Stoughton family provided the spark. Elizabeth Stoughton, a first cousin once removed from the Abigail Stoughton who had caused so much trouble in the 1720s, neglected to obtain her father's permission when she married Joseph Diggens in 1740. Diggens was a reputable man but was undesirable because he came from one of Windsor's relatively poorer families. Elizabeth's father brought his objections to Timothy Edwards, still pastor of East Windsor parish, and Edwards denied communion to the errant Diggens and refused to baptize their child. The parishioners protested that they should have had a role in making this decision, once again raising the issue of ministerial control. The conflict grew to such lengths that Edwards completely halted communion for three years. The problem was finally resolved by the intervention of the Hartford North Association, the same group that had heard William Thrall's complaints.[110]

Conclusion

The Thrall family saga dramatizes the interconnectedness of family and community problems in early eighteenth-century Connecticut and suggests that historians should continue to investigate the nature of the connection. Family problems such as those of the Thralls and Stoughtons obviously drew the larger community into their struggle by extending the conflict to a major social institution, the church. The impact of the Thrall family crisis was more subtle than the Stoughton case but perhaps no less important to the people of Windsor. The incident forced members of the community to take sides by voting in church and by testifying—or not testifying—before civil authorities.

Friends and neighbors were inevitably caught up in the family dispute because of the way eighteenth-century Connecticut towns dealt with problems. Initial attempts were informal and remained within the community: persuasion by relatives and neighbors, arbitration by mutually agreed upon mediators, and moral appeals by minister and congregation. When these methods failed, the community went to higher, outside authorities, first to the ministers' association and then to the courts. Family affairs thus became community and even colonywide concerns; private and public worlds were conflated. In a New England town that still upheld the ideal, if not the reality, of a moral, harmonious community, even disruption within a single family could not remain a private matter. This minor family squabble became a major community disruption, aggravating old feuds and tensions and giving rise to new ones, both within the Thralls' extended family and between families.[111]

A profile of the Thralls' witnesses indicates definite patterns of mutual support in Windsor quite different from Nancy Cott's findings in her statistical analysis of Massachusetts divorces. Cott found that couples seeking divorces relied overwhelmingly on non-relatives rather than on relatives as witnesses and that both spouses had more male than female witnesses.[112] By using the case study method, we can establish relationships that Cott would have been unable to discover, since she relied only on last names and relationships actually stated in the depositions. We can also see connections other than blood relationships that may help explain why certain people turned to each other for help.

At least half of Hannah's witnesses were relatives: her mother, her two unmarried sisters, and two probable first cousins, one of whom was William's former servant. Another witness was the daughter of a woman who was herself suing for divorce. Hannah's other witnesses were a local minister and the son of a local constable. William had a smaller percentage of relatives among his supporters, about a quarter, including his mother, his younger brother, and two first cousins, both similarly related to Hannah. His other deponents were a married couple who lived on a neighboring farm, two men from out of town who might have been involved in business with him, and a former servant to Hannah's father. His eight remaining deponents were all unmarried men in their late teens or early twenties, possibly members of the militia company that had elected him their captain.

Half of Hannah's witnesses were women, but only two of William's seventeen were women, his mother and a next-door neighbor. The testimony in the Thrall case indicates that Hannah and other Windsor women moved mainly in a circle of women, while William carried on most of his activities among men. The younger men seem to have spent most of their time in all-male groups, whether working in the fields, walking home from work, visiting friends, or carousing. The women shared household chores, child care, and visiting. Among the Thralls and their friends, separate men's and women's spheres existed well before such an ideology solidified nearly a hundred years later.[113]

Besides furthering our understanding of women's daily lives, the Thrall case can help us investigate the legal position of women in colonial Connecticut. Historians have often used the attitude of the law as a means of defining colonial women's status.[114] However, far more went into court decisions than simply defined ideas of women's place. The key to the Thrall decision, as we have seen, was a typically convoluted Puritan interpretation of Biblical law. According to the statutes, William clearly should have won his case. That he did not has little or nothing to do with the judges' compassion or sense of justice for women in general and far more to do with the specific circumstances of the case: William did not live up to Puritan concepts of a husband's responsibilities. Eventually, the law books incorporated the principle established in *Thrall* v.

Thrall—that a husband who drove his wife away was himself to be considered the deserter.[115] Only through more detailed case histories can we begin to understand why women, as well as men, lost some court cases and won others and what the reality of women's legal status—as opposed to its statutory definition—actually was, and how it evolved.

Case studies using divorce records can thus provide valuable insights into women's relationship with the law and with their communities. By looking more closely at colonial divorce records in conjunction with other documents, historians should be able to illuminate the intricate, hidden ties between women and institutions, women and families, and family and community crises.

REFERENCES

This essay was originally a master's essay written at Columbia University under the direction of Eric L. McKitrick (1981). In addition to Professor McKitrick and the members of the master's seminar, I would like to thank the following for their advice on various drafts: Carol Berkin, Cornelia Dayton, Linda Kerber, Peter S. Onuf, Rosalind Rosenberg, Herbert Sloan, and Alden T. Vaughan. I would also like to thank Eunice Gillman Dibella of the Connecticut State Library.

1. Depositions of George Bradley (September 9, 1736) and John Stoughton (May 25, 1737), *Thrall v. Thrall,* Connecticut Superior Court Files, Hartford District, Divorce 1740–95, Connecticut State Library, Hartford (hereafter abbreviated *Thrall v. Thrall;* other cases known as *Thrall v. Thrall* will be given full citations); J. Hammond Trumbull and Charles J. Hoadley, eds., *The Public Records of the Colony of Connecticut . . . ,* 15 vols. (Hartford, 1850–1890), vol. 5, p. 396. Dates throughout are given in old style, but with years stated as though they began on January 1. For quotations from manuscript sources I have followed the "expanded method" in Frank Freidel, ed., *Harvard Guide to American History,* 2d. ed. rev. (Cambridge, 1974), pp. 28–31. All manuscript sources cited are located in the Connecticut State Library, Hartford.

2. The couple's fathers were brothers. All genealogical information is derived from the Barbour Collection of Town Vital Records, and Henry R. Stiles, *The History and Genealogy of Ancient Windsor, Connecticut,* 2 vols. (Hartford, 1891).

3. Trumbull and Hoadley, *Public Records,* vol. 2, p. 328.

4. For colonial divorce in general, see Nelson M. Blake, *The Road to Reno: A History of Divorce in the United States* (New York, 1962), chap. 4. For Connecticut, see Henry S. Cohn, "Connecticut's Divorce Mechanism, 1636–1969," *American Journal of Legal History* 14 (1970): 35–54; Sheldon S. Cohen, " 'To Parts of the World Unknown': The Circumstances of Divorce in Connecticut, 1750–1797," *Canadian Review of American Studies* 11 (1980): 275–93; and Linda Kerber, *Women of the Republic: Intellect and Ideology in Revolutionary America* (Chapel Hill, N.C., 1980), pp. 159–83. Cohen's figures indicate that there were at least a thousand divorce cases in eighteenth-century Connecticut. Massachusetts was a poor second, with 229 cases from 1692 to 1786. See Nancy F. Cott, "Divorce and the Changing Status of Women

in Eighteenth-Century Massachusetts," *William and Mary Quarterly*, 3d ser., no. 33 (1976): 587. Massachusetts required petitioners to appear in person at court in Boston, while the Connecticut court rode circuit, hearing cases in four, and later eight, county seats, an obvious advantage in an age of poor transportation.

5. Petition of Thomas Thrall, *Thrall v. Thrall*, Connecticut Archives, Private Controversies, 2d. ser., vol. 7.

6. Richard B. Morris, "Women's Rights in Early American Law," in *Studies in the History of American Law* (1930; reprint ed., New York, 1958), pp. 162–63.

7. Kerber, *Women of the Republic*, p. 162. In 1843 "habitual intemperance" and "intolerable cruelty" were added to the statutes as grounds for divorce.

8. Town studies that have virtually ignored the presence of women include Philip J. Greven, Jr., *Four Generations: Population Land, and Family in Colonial Andover, Massachusetts* (Ithaca, N.Y., 1954) and Bruce C. Daniels, *The Connecticut Town: Growth and Development, 1635–1790* (Middletown, Conn., 1979). Robert A. Gross, *The Minutemen and Their World* (New York, 1976) devotes a scant six pages to the role of women in Concord. Recent books on eighteenth-century women contain many useful insights but are still confined by their sources to the literate minority. For example, see Nancy F. Cott, *The Bonds of Womanhood: "Woman's Sphere" in New England, 1780–1835;* and Mary Beth Norton, *Liberty's Daughters: The Revolutionary Experience of American Women, 1750–1800* (Boston, 1980). One recent book uses court records extensively: Laurel Thatcher Ulrich, *Good Wives: Image and Reality in the Lives of Women in Northern New England, 1650–1750* (New York, 1982).

9. Nancy F. Cott, "Eighteenth-Century Family and Social Life Revealed in Massachusetts Divorce Records," *Journal of Social History* 10 (1976): 20–44: idem, "Divorce and the Changing Status of Women."

10. The only other type of court cases in which women figured prominently were prosecutions of "female" crimes like fornication and infanticide. See Lyle Koehler, *A Search for Power: The "Weaker Sex" in Seventeenth-Century New England* (Urbana, Ill., 1980), esp. pp. 189–215.

11. For recent works that analyze the application of statutes see David Thomas Konig, *Law and Society in Puritan Massachusetts: Essex County, 1629–1692* (Chapel Hill, N.C., 1979) and William E. Nelson, *Dispute and Conflict Resolution in Plymouth County, Massachusetts, 1725–1825* (Chapel Hill, N.C., 1981).

12. Barbour Collection of Town Vital Records.

13. Alan Macfarlane, *The Family Life of Ralph Josselin* (Cambridge, 1970), p. 11. Two important works that mine legal records for evidence of everyday life are Emmanuel Le Roy Ladurie, trans. Barbara Bray (New York, 1978) and Jonathan D. Spence, *The Death of Woman Wang* (New York, 1978).

14. Kathryn Kish Sklar calls her *Catharine Beecher: A Study in American Domesticity* (New York, 1973), "an effort to use the biographical density and motivational impulses of one person to uncover and isolate significant questions about the relationship between women and American society" (p. xiv).

15. For the early history of Windsor, see Stiles, *Ancient Windsor*, vol. 1, pp. 17–171. The population estimate is extrapolated from Evarts B. Greene and Virginia D. Harrington, *American Population before the Federal Census of 1790* (New York, 1932), pp. 53, 58–59.

16. Linda Auwers Bissell, "Family, Friends, and Neighbors: Social Interaction in Seventeenth-Century Windsor, Connecticut" (Ph.D. diss., Brandeis University, 1973), pp. 172–73.

17. Ibid., pp. 26, 130, 177; Stiles, *Ancient Windsor*, vol. 1, pp. 70, 132, 138; Trumbull and Hoadley, *Public Records*, vol. 2, pp. 150, 193; Bissell, "Seventeenth-Century Windsor," p. 173.

18. Trumbull and Hoadley, *Public Records,* vol. 3, pp. 72, 193; Stiles, *Ancient Windsor,* vol. 1, pp. 139, 213.

19. Trumbull and Hoadley, *Public Records,* vol. 5, p. 43; will of Timothy Thrall (1724), inventory of Timothy Thrall estate (1725), Probate Files.

20. Will of Timothy Thrall, Probate Files.

21. Toby Lee Ditz, "Ownership and Obligation: Family and Inheritance in Five Connecticut Towns, 1750–1820" (Ph.D. diss., Columbia University, 1982), p. 188. Also see Windsor wills in Charles W. Manwaring, *A Digest of the Early Connecticut Probate Records,* 3 vols. (Hartford, 1904–6).

22. The average widowhood was seven to ten years, according to Alexander Keyssar, "Widowhood in Eighteenth-Century Massachusetts," *Perspectives in American History* 8 (1974): 92–93.

23. Will of Timothy Thrall (1724), Inventory of Timothy Thrall estate (1725), Probate Files.

24. The divorce records show that Hannah had a sister named Elizabeth, Jr., but her birth was never recorded.

25. Charity was said to be thirteen in 1738. See Probate Court Records, vol. 13, p. 38.

26. Records remain only for Thomas Thrall's offense, not Hannah's. Connecticut Archives, Crimes and Misdemeanors, 1st ser., vol. 3, pp. 81–84. For premarital sex in colonial America, see Daniel Scott Smith and Michael Hindus, "Premarital Pregnancy in America, 1640–1971: An Overview and Interpretation," *Journal of Marriage and the Family* 5 (1975): 537–70.

27. Stiles, *Ancient Windsor,* vol. 2, p. 762.

28. George Elliott Howard, *A History of Matrimonial Institutions . . . ,* vol. 2, p. 213.

29. John Demos, *A Little Commonwealth: Family Life in Plymouth Colony* (New York, 1970), pp. 68, 133; Ulrich, *Good Wives,* pp. 138–144. Two-year intervals between births are, of course, the usual premodern pattern.

30. Deposition of Eunice Stoughton (May 1737), *Thrall v. Thrall.*

31. Ibid., deposition of John Thrall (September 27, 1736).

32. Inventory of William Thrall estate (1738), Probate Files, lists the four adult slaves along with two children.

33. Judgment of Stephen Mix, Samuel Whitman, Benjamin Cotton, and Timothy Edwards (February 26, 1734), copy filed as evidence in *Thrall v. Thrall.*

34. Deposition of Sarah Thrall (September 23, 1736); Depositions of George Bradley and John Stoughton, *Thrall v. Thrall.*

35. Trumbull and Hoadley, *Public Records,* vol. 7, p. 399. For usual procedures in appointing officers, see Daniels, *Connecticut Town,* pp. 134–35.

36. William's carefully written petitions in his own handwriting demonstrate a high level of literacy. His commercial activities took him often to court. See, for example, note 73 below.

37. Kerber, *Women of the Republic,* p. 160.

38. For English marriage and divorce practice, see Howard, *History of Matrimonial Institutions,* vol. 1, pp. 253–364; and Chilton L. Powell, *English Domestic Relations, 1487–1653* (New York, 1917).

39. *Spencer v. Spencer, Smith v. Cole, Slate v. Slate,* Connecticut Archives, Crimes and Misdemeanors, 1st ser., vol. 3, pp. 256–58, 284–86, 304. For the remaining two cases, see below, notes 41 and 43.

40. Kerber, *Women of the Republic,* p. 173; Nelson, *Dispute and Conflict Resolution,* pp. 26–43.

41. *Moore v. Stoughton* (1725), Connecticut Superior Court Files, Hartford Dis-

trict, Divorce, 1740–1795. See also Stiles, *Ancient Windsor,* vol. 1, pp. 569–70; and John A. Stoughton, *"Windsor Farmes": A Glimpse of an Old Parish* (Hartford, 1883), pp. 71–72. For the divorce case of Richard Edwards, Timothy's father, see Connecticut Archives, Crimes and Misdemeanors, 1st ser., vol. 3, pp. 235–38; and Ola Winslow, *Jonathan Edwards* (New York, 1940), pp. 18–20.

42. *Probate Records,* vol. 2, pp. 263–64.

43. Deposition of Hannah Newberry Merriman (undated), *Merriman* v. *Merriman,* 1718, Connecticut Superior Court Files, New Haven District, Divorce, 1712–1798, (hereafter *Merriman* v. *Merriman).*

44. Deposition of Joseph Benham, Abraham Downhill, Mary Downhill, Hannah Tomson, Sara Doolittle, and Mary Daton (March 7, 1718), *Merriman* v. *Merriman;* John Merriman to Hannah Merriman (1714), *Merriman* v. *Merriman.* On putting out children, see Morgan, *Puritan Family,* pp. 68–78; Demos, *A Little Commonwealth,* pp. 71–75.

45. Judgment of seven ministers (1717), *Merriman* v. *Merriman.*

46. Morgan, *Puritan Family,* pp. 39–48.

47. Judgment of seven ministers, *Merriman* v. *Merriman.*

48. Superior Court at New Haven (September 9, 1718), Connecticut Superior Court Records, vol. 2.

49. Nelson, *Dispute and Conflict Resolution,* pp. 26–43.

50. Judgment of Macks, Whitman, Cotton, and Edwards, *Thrall* v. *Thrall.* On spouses living separately, see Morgan, *Puritan Family,* pp. 38–40.

51. Deposition of Elizabeth Thrall (October 14, 1734), *Thrall* v. *Thrall.*

52. The only document bearing Hannah's name, her will, was signed with a mark, indicating that she was probably illiterate. For discussions of literacy, see Linda Auwers, "The Social Meaning of Female Literacy: Windsor, Connecticut, 1660–1775," *Newberry [Library] Papers in Family and Community History* (1977); and Kenneth A. Lockridge, *Literacy in Colonial New England* (New York, 1974).

53. Deposition of Israel Ashley (September 15, 1736), *Thrall* v. *Thrall.*

54. Zephanian Swift, *A System of the Laws of the State of Connecticut* (Windham, Connecticut, 1795), vol. 1, p. 212.

55. Deposition of Elizabeth Thrall, *Thrall* v. *Thrall.*

56. On women's childrearing responsibilities, see Norton, *Liberty's Daughters,* pp. 102–3. For the view that fathers spent a great deal of time with their children, see John Demos's comments in *New York Times,* May 17, 1982, p. B10.

57. Deposition of Elizabeth Thrall, *Thrall* v. *Thrall.*

58. Morgan, *Puritan Family,* pp. 41–42; Ulrich, *Good Wives,* pp. 108–9; Morris, "Women's Rights," pp. 166–73.

59. Deposition of Sarah Thrall; Deposition of Thomas Moses (October 7, 1736), *Thrall* v. *Thrall.*

60. Ibid., deposition of Othniel Gillet (September 28, 1736).

61. Ibid., deposition of Timothy Edwards (September 9, 1735); Judgment of Mix, Whitman, Cotton, and Edwards.

62. Ibid.

63. Petition of Thomas Thrall, *Thrall* v. *Thrall,* Connecticut Archives, Private Controversies, 2d ser., vol. 27, pp. 161–68.

64. Morgan, *Puritan Family,* pp. 66–67.

65. Petition of Thomas Thrall, *Thrall* v. *Thrall,* Connecticut Archives, Private Controversies, 2d ser., vol. 27, pp. 161–68. For similar failures of informal arbitration, see Nelson, *Dispute and Conflict Resolution,* p. 14.

66. Deposition of Samuel Palmer (October 2, 1736), *Thrall* v. *Thrall.*

67. Ibid., deposition of Moses Griswold (May 1737).

68. Ibid., deposition of Elizabeth Thrall, Jr., and Aaron Pinney (October 7, 1736).

69. Ibid.; Deposition of Samuel Palmer; Deposition of Abigail Stevens, Jr. (October 4, 1736), *Thrall v. Thrall.*

70. Ibid., petition of William Thrall (August 25, 1735); Deposition of Timothy Edwards.

71. Ibid., petition of William Thrall.

72. *Thrall* v. *Owen, Thrall* v. *Winchell,* Superior Court at Hartford (September 9, 1735), Superior Court Records, vol. 7.

73. Deposition of Timothy Thrall (September 28, 1736), *Thrall* v. *Thrall.*

74. Manwaring, *Probate Records, passim.*

75. Will of William Thrall (1736, probated 1738), Probate Files.

76. Inventory of Sarah Thrall estate (1741), Probate Files.

77. Manwaring, *Probate Records, passim.* Although formal compliments in legal documents are poor indications of the presence of affection, their omission may well indicate its absence.

78. Morris, "Women's Rights," p. 157; Ditz, "Ownership and Obligation," p. 171.

79. Will of William Thrall, Probate Files; Manwaring, *Probate Records, passim.*

80. Will of William Thrall, Probate Files.

81. Deposition of Abraham Pinney and Abel Griswold (May 1737), *Thrall* v. *Thrall.* Abraham Pinney was the son of William and Hannah's aunt Martha, who had married Nathaniel Pinney.

82. Ibid., deposition of Noadiah Phelps (March 31, 1737).

83. Ibid., deposition of John Owen, Jr. (September 30, 1736).

84. David H. Flaherty, *Privacy in Colonial New England* (Charlottesville, Va.), pp. 76–79.

85. Deposition of Benjamin Griswold, Jr. (May 1737), *Thrall* v. *Thrall.*

86. For example, Ibid., deposition of Samuel Palmer.

87. Scott and Hindus, "Premarital Pregnancy," pp. 556–58.

88. Noadiah and Sarah married September 29, 1737; the baby was born November 29. Sarah was the first cousin once removed of John Owen, Jr., who had accused her future husband of adultery.

89. Depositions of George Bradley and John Stoughton, *Thrall* v. *Thrall.*

90. Petition of Abigail Stevens (1736), *Stevens* v. *Stevens,* Superior Court Files, Hartford District, Divorce, 1740–1795.

91. Deposition of John Thrall, *Thrall* v. *Thrall.*

92. Ibid., deposition of Samuel Palmer.

93. Ibid., depositions of Abigail Stevens, Jr., and Samuel Palmer.

94. Superior Court at Hartford (May 25, 1737), Superior Court Records, vol. 7.

95. Petition of William Thrall (March 1, 1738), *Thrall* v. *Thrall.*

96. Petition of Esther Griswold, *Griswold* v. *Thrall,* Connecticut Archives, Crimes and Misdemeanors, 2d ser., vol. 4, pp. 44–45. On accusations of fatherhood, see Swift, *System of the Laws,* vol. 1, pp. 208–10.

97. Probate Court Records, vol. 13, p. 38.

98. Children could choose their own guardians when they reached the age of discretion, or puberty, defined as fourteen for boys and twelve for girls. See Swift, *System of the Laws,* vol. 1, p. 213.

99. Distribution of William Thrall estate (1740), Probate Files.

100. The only land Hickox left at his death was outside Windsor, in Goshen and Barkhempsted. Distribution of Joseph Hickox estate (1747), Probate Files.

101. Inventory of Jonathan Alford estate (1779), Probate Files.

102. Distribution of Joseph Hickox estate (1747), Probate Files; Manwaring, *Probate Records*, vol. 3, p. 568.

103. James Cornish was the son of Hannah and William's aunt Elizabeth, who had married James Cornish, Sr., of Simsbury.

104. Noah Phelps, *History of Simsbury, Granby, and Canton* (Hartford, 1845), p. 156.

105. Will of Hannah Thrall (1779, probated 1779), Probate Files.

106. *Stevens* v. *Stevens* (1736), *Porter* v. *Rockwell* (1737), *Gaylord* v. *Copley* (1739), *Bliss* v. *Mugleston* (1742), *Hodge* v. *Hodge* (1742), *Drake* v. *Holcomb* (1744), *Holaday* v. *Holaday* (1746), *Moore* v. *Soper* (1747), and *Wright* v. *Doolittle* (1748), Superior Court Files, Hartford District, Divorce, 1740–1795.

107. Ibid., *Hodge* v. *Hodge* (1751) and *Person* v. *Person* (1753).

108. For estimates of the divorce rate in Connecticut, 1750–1800, see Cohen, "Divorce in Connecticut," p. 290.

109. Cott, "Divorce and the Changing Status of Women," p. 593, also mentions this phenomenon.

110. Stiles, *Ancient Windsor*, vol. 1. pp. 570–74; Richard Bushman, *From Puritan to Yankee: Character and the Social Order in Connecticut, 1690–1795* (Cambridge, Mass., 1962), p. 161.

111. Compare with Michael Zuckerman, *Peaceable Kingdoms: New England Towns in the Eighteenth Century* (New York, 1970).

112. Cott. "Family and Social Life," pp. 24–26.

113. Compare Cott, *Bonds of Womanhood;* Gerda Lerner, "The Lady and the Mill Girl: Changes in the Status of Women in the Age of Jackson, 1800–1840," *Midcontinent American Studies Journal* 10 (1969):5–14.

114. For example, Morris, "Women's Rights"; Marylynn Salmon, "The Property of Women in Early America: A Comparative Study" (Ph.D. diss., Bryn Mawr College, 1980).

115. Henry Dutton, ed., *A Revision of Swift's Digest of the Laws of Connecticut* (New Haven, 1853), vol. 1, p. 21.

INDEX

Adultery, 43–44,51–53,56–63
Affective relationships, 3
Allyn family, 47
Allyn, Henry, 58,63
Amelia County, 6,13,14,15,16,17,20, 21,22,23,27,29,30,32,33,34
Ames, William, 56
Anglican Church, 7,11,32
Arbitration, 57,68

Barnett, Mary, 32
Beard, Mary, 8
Bedford County, 24,25
Bigamy, 44
Bine, Sarah, 29
Blackstone, Sir William, 11
Blue Ridge Mountains, 13
Booker, Edmund, 22
Booker, Judith (mother), 34
Booker, Judith (daughter), 34
Bristol Parish Vestry, 32
Bush River, 15
Byrd, William, II, 14

Carr, Lois, 1,5,6,17
Carter, John, 26
Carter, Landon, 7
Carter, William, 26
Catholics, 12
Chapman, Samuel, 9
Chapman, Unity (Mrs. Loving), 9
Children: care of, 55; custody of, 56; number of, 49; putting out of, 52. *See also* Family, Inheritance; Wills, Women.
Common Law, 7,8,9,10,11,12,15
Community, 3,44–46,67–68,70
Connecticut Colony: divorce laws, 43,51; General Assembly, 47,50, 52,57,66; Superior Court, 52,58, 62–64

Constables, 48
Cobb, Edith, 21,32–33,34
Cobb, John, 33
Cobb, Judith, 33
Cobb, Samuel (father), 21,32,33
Cobb, Samuel (son), 21
Cobb, Theodosia, 33
Cooke, Abraham (father), 30
Cooke, Abraham (son), 30
Cooke, Mary, 30
Cott, Nancy,45,58
Coverture, 8,13,26
Crenshaw, Elkanah, 22
Crowder, Dorothy, 34

Deen, James, 6
Desertion, 43–44,51–59
Divorce, 3,12,43–44,45,51–53,56,59, 63–64,67,68,69
Dower, 10,15,16,17,20,21,27,44,60,66

East Windsor Parish, 51,56,67
Edmonson, Benjamin, 15
Edmonson, Constant, 15
Edmonson, Mary, 15
Edmonson, Upton, 15
Edwards, Jonathan, 52
Edwards, Timothy, 51–52,56,59,67
Ellyson, Gerard, 26
Ellyson, Sarah, 26
Equity, 8–9
Executors, 22,23,60,65
Executrixes, 22–24,25,32,33

Family, 3,6,7,9,10,11,13,14,15–21,24, 25,26,31,45–46,66–70
Fee Simple, 20,21
Feme Covert, 8,9,13
Feme Sole, 8,24,26,28
Finney, Mary, 34
Fornication, 44,48,62,64–65